Quit complaining! When I was your age, the snow was deeper, the summers were hotter, the fish were bigger, we had no TV or electronic games, practically nothing to eat, and we had to walk two miles every morning to school.

Life was really tough in the 'dirty 30s', living in the slums of North Bay, Ontario, near one of Canada's largest hobo jungles. And we loved it!

Down by the Railroad Tracks
by Cal Smith

A portrait of life in the 'good old days'
especially for my treasured family and friends

Calsbooks Publishing

Calsbooks Publishing
103 – 9005 Centaurus Circle,
Burnaby, B.C. V3J 7N4
www.calsbooks.com
1.604.728-6325

In the USA
1577 D St. #11
Blaine, Wa 98230
360-567-6860

© 2010 Cal Smith All Rights Reserved

No part of this book may be reproduced, stored in a retrieval system, or transmitted by any means without the written permission of the author.

First published by Calsbooks Publications 12/21/2010

ISBN – 978-0-9812560-6-1

Library & Archives Canada/ Bibliotheque & Archives Canada

Printed in the USA

CONTENT

Introduction	5
The Best Man	9
Getaway	27
The Nigger	39
Singing to the Bears	45
Holy Rolling	49
Earthquake	53
Serial Killer	57
Polio	63
Wrong Side of the Tracks	69
Suicide Trick	73
The Hobo Jungle	75
The Bull Fight	91
Long Arm of the Law	95
Guns and Whistles	105
Paddy's Lakeside Casino	111
The Dionne Legacy	121
The Honey Wagon	125
The Plague	131
Quicksand	139

INTRODUCTION

It is no wonder that history teachers put so much emphasis on the dates, statistics, and generalities of important historical events, rather than on the specifics. History is largely fiction, with the details of events distorted, obscured, and restructured according to the biases, prejudices, and self-interests of the recording historian.

No two people ever see anything from the same perspective. Thus, my view of life in Northern Ontario during the 'dirty 30s' and war-torn 40s are from 'the wrong side of the tracks' where the houses are small and shabby, with garbage littered lawns, outdoor toilets, and trains screaming within yards of our beds at all times of day and night. They would be very different from the impressions of Rita Rivelis, the pretty little girl who sat next to me in my first year of elementary school and who usually paid for my chocolate milk in the school milk program.

Living, as she did, in a mansion-like three story red brick house with elegant white columns and shutters, and filled with expensive mahogany and oak furniture, imported carpets on the floors, and signed oil paintings on the walls, she had no idea we were in the midst of a world-wide recession.

She didn't know there were parts of the city where large families were crowded into bed-bug infested shacks, or ate off of stained, cracked dinnerware, sitting at home-made tables on unmatched rickety wooden chairs purchased for pennies on the dollar from the second-hand stores on Oak Street. How could her memories of life in the 1930s be anything remotely like mine?

Unlike Rita's father, Nate, who owned a successful footwear store, my dad, like millions of other uneducated and unskilled Canadian workers, was almost always without work. Worse still, he was almost always sick. He had one kidney that poisoned his system and eventually developed an abscess and had to be removed. So, while my family moved from one low-rent house to another, Rita lived comfortably at one address in the elite section of the city near the school we both attended.

By the time I was seven we were resident in a four-room frame house without hot water or an indoor bathroom. We literally had 'no pot to pee in' – we used empty cans conveniently placed under the edge of our beds for emergency use in the dark of night and dead of winter. My parents slept in one bedroom. The rest of us – two sisters and a brother – slept in the other. In those pre-adolescent years we had yet to learn there is a difference between boys and girls

To say that we lived on the wrong side of the tracks wouldn't be entirely correct. The Canadian National Railway dissected the city into north/south sections, with the richer folk dominating the south central section. The Canadian Pacific paralleled the lake shore from one end of town to the other. And the T&NO (Temiskaming and Northern Ontario) railway headed out to James Bay in the far north from its yards in the east end.

Many poor people lived in various locations around the fringes of the city, but the real slums and hobo jungles were in a small area in the extreme west end, parallel to, and within slingshot reach, of the CNR tracks that sliced through the city's center.

The trains roaring into town less than a hundred feet from the house were more of an excitement than annoyance as far as we kids were concerned. The engineers would acknowledge us with a special blast of their horns as they neared the

Timmins Street crossing. They always waved, and sometimes threw candies to us. There was another big advantage in having the tracks so close to us: we could make really neat knife blades by laying various sized headless spikes on the rails for the trains to flatten as they passed. All we had to do then was drive them into carved wooden handles and sharpen one edge.

One of the country's largest hobo jungles was only five blocks south of our house, close to the lake. But it was more like a wooded paddock in a wildlife preserve than it was a jungle. The first and only time I visited there, I had the impression that I had just stumbled upon Robin Hood's camp in Sherwood Forest. It was a small clearing in the center of a four-acre wooded area near the bottom end of Timmins Street.

Rita's family wasn't the only one that lived quite comfortably during the depression. Businessmen, professionals, and railroad workers experienced none of the hardships suffered by the unemployed masses – particularly those who were forced to leave home and sneak rides on boxcars to look for work. The contrast between North Bay's elite and the hobos was sharpened by the fact that only a few blocks separated the crude hobo jungle from the luxurious homes of wealthy lawyers, doctors, railroad executives, politicians, realtors, and businessmen. The accounts of the genteel life these people enjoyed in those days wouldn't be anything close to what you will read in this book – or from the tales spun by the rail riding survivors of the dirty thirties.

Keep in mind though that memory is not reality. Recollections are often distorted and riddled with holes that must be filled in with reconstructions based on unrelated but similar events, places, or objects. Other times what we think are memories are really just stories we heard somewhere in the distant past and may or may not have any credibility. In fact, most memories of 'the old days' have been greatly warped and exaggerated from the telling and retelling, again and again, by parents and siblings.

There's also the question of being able to trust your own eyes. We all like to think we have good memories – particularly of events that are unique or dramatic – but we don't.

For example, in 1980 a bomb exploded in an Italian train station killing 85 people. It stopped the station clock at 10:25 am. The clock was later repaired and worked perfectly for 16 years. When it stopped a second time, it wasn't repaired but the hands were set permanently to 10:25 as a memorial of the 1980 terrorist attack. Researchers then asked 180 people who worked in the station, or were intimately familiar with it, how long the clock had read 10:25. All but 20 said it had been that way since the explosion.

So all I can promise to readers of this book, is that I will try to leave you with a realistic impression of life as I knew it in the thirties and forties in Northern Ontario. It was a time and place like no other and would be lost forever without someone to tell of it, and I mismember it perfectly.

In short, the ink with which I write this story is *'a homogenized mixture of memory, emotion, and unintentional lies'.*

Chapter One
THE BEST MAN

I was born in Tonnawanda, New York, on Aug 3rd, 1930 at a time when the Gallea brothers were in tight control of the whiskey and gambling business in Buffalo, as part of the 'Five (mafioso) Families of New York'. A year later, my parents, Herman and Ruth Smith vacated our Tonnawanda apartment a scant three hours before two men with 'Chicago Typewriters' broke down the door with intent to splatter the walls with our blood.

After what my parents did to Dad's youngest brother two years earlier, that's about the only thing that could have made them return to North Bay, where they had left a stirred-up hornet's nest of angry relatives who would have revelled at the news that we had all been punctured with .45 caliber holes in our Tonnawanda apartment.

I'll explain the reason for the family's deep, smoldering hatred in the next few pages, but the reason why they had to leave Tonnawanda so suddenly is another story that spans more than ten years, and will have to wait for publication of my next book "Escape to Obscurity".

You couldn't blame dad's family for hating him – and my mom -- but I was after-the-fact to the whole thing. How could anybody hate a one-year-old baby? If I had been there when it happened, I propably would have felt just as angry and contemptuous of them for what they did! What kind of man would accept an invitation to be the best man at his brother's wedding, then run away with the (almost) bride, leaving the groom humiliated, bewildered and betrayed, crying on the church steps.

How could anybody do such a thing to his own brother? For that matter, how could a bride-to-be leave her betrothed at the alter to run away with a man she had met only two days earlier? Actually, my mother did more than just run away with him. She precipitated the whole thing. She enticed him into leaving and taking her with him!

But I'm getting ahead of myself.

Dad and his friend Joe Ranger, had crossed into the United States at Niagara Falls illegally in June, 1925, and moved into an apartment in Buffalo. Once settled in, they immediately contacted Salvatore Callea who, with his brother Vincenzo, controlled the booze and gambling business in Buffalo and Tonnawanda for the New York Mafioso.

Michael McRae, a disbarred Texas lawyer friend of dad, then living in North Bay, had pre-arranged an introduction with Salvatore, ostensibly to secure employment for them. The meeting took place in a quiet booth in the Callea Restaurant at 369 Connecticut Street in Buffalo.

Salvatore was impressed with the two men and agreed to give them day jobs at mob-owned businesses. Herman would pack shingles at the Creo-Dipt plant in Tonnawanda. Joe would make sand molds for heavy machinery parts at Buffalo Steel Castings Inc. Dad would have a half-hour commute to the shingle factory, but his wages would be high enough to make it well worth while.

Post-war Life in New York state was exciting. The two

friends worked hard at their jobs during the day, and played hard at night in speak-easies and gambling joints in Niagara Falls, Tonnawanda, and Buffalo. Dad seldom wrote to his mother, but often sent small gifts and notes to his young sister Dorothy. She'd suffered with rickets as a baby and had never been able to walk without breaking her legs.

Then, one day in May, 1929, he got a letter from his mother asking him to come home to be the best man at Gordon's wedding. He had been wanting to go home and see Dorothy for some time now anyway, and it would also give him a chance to talk over a business idea with Michael McRae. He wrote back agreeing to be home on June 13, two days before the wedding.

"Hello Mother,

You didn't say who Gordon was marrying. Is it the same girl you mentioned at Christmas? I don't remember her name now. But it doesn't matter, I'll find out soon enough.

I'll be there on Thursday, June 13th. Joe Ranger is going to drive me so I am not sure exactly what time we'll arrive, but probably before 9am. We plan on going to Toronto on the morning of the 12th and should be leaving there about midnight.

Give my best wishes to Gordon and tell Dorothy I love her.

Love,

Herman."

When the day arrived, Joe drove dad to Toronto but changed his mind about going all the way up north. They'd had a meeting with a friend in Toronto, and Joe was anxious to introduce him to Callea brothers in Buffalo. So Herman rented a car at the CPR station and drove alone to North Bay arriving shortly before Midnight. He checked into the Continental Hotel for the night and was at his mother's house on East Main street by nine the following morning.

The house was one of the finest in the city's east end, a grand, three-story red brick building with an enclosed front entrance, and white trim throughout. He had often stayed here before he went to the States, but it had always amazed him that his mother had come so far from the shack they had lived in deep in the woods of Widdifield Township.

"It's too bad my bastard father can't see this place and know just how well she was able to do without him to drag her down," he thought as he rang the doorbell.

He hated Blakeney Smith, his father, leaving Owen Sound where they were all happy and taking them north into the wilderness just as the first world war was starting. It wouldn't even have been so bad if he had chosen to settle near the 'Station' where there was a school, a small store, and a few homes and where getting back and forth to town was fairly easy. The T&NO trains didn't make regular stops there, but they could be flagged down if there were passengers waiting to get on.

Instead of that. He moved them into a shack two miles into the bush, on a road that was little more than a deer trail. What was he thinking? There was no way to make a living away out there. Two other families had almost died trying. The land was too rocky to cultivate and the trees too small to cut for timber.

There were no jobs, no neighbors, and no welfare. If they ran out of flour and potatoes, they'd starve. If they ran short of wood in the winter time, they would freeze to death – which wouldn't take long in the extreme cold of the north in those days.

There was no pump on the well, so water had to be dipped out with a pail tied onto the end of a rope. It work enough in the summer, but in winter, the well froze so deep and solid, it was almost impossible to keep a hole open large enough for the pail. It was all they could do to chisel out a hole big enough for a small jam can with the heavy eight-foot-long iron ice pick. Even then, it was a trick to lower the can into the hole and tip it enough to fill with water. By the time the pails were filled and carried to the house, noses, ears, and finger tips would be dangerously close to frost bite.

The outhouse posed another serious problem. In the wintertime they couldn't get to it without spending an hour shoveling a pathway through the deep snow that seemed to fall continuously from October to mid March. If they did shovel a path, there was a problem digging deep enough in front of the door to get it open. Then they faced the ordeal of baring their their rear ends over a seat caked with iced pee – or worse.

A better alternative was to clear a narrow path to the side of the house and squat there. When that spot became too disgusting to use any more, it was simply a matter of shoveling another narrow path to another location -- as close as possible to the house of course. It gets cold out there!

It was actually quite convenient in one way. When all of the catalog pages were used up, snowballs were always handy and did the job admirably well. It was a reasonable substitute for the weekly baths they wouldn't be able to enjoy until the weather warmed up in April or May.

Unfortunately, they had to pay for all this convenience when spring rolled around and the snow melted to expose the piles of poop that stacked all over the yard, as if a large colony of huge dung gophers had been busy building multi-level homes under the ground. Five people can produce an awful lot of waste in four months.

As it turned out, toiletry wasn't much more pleasant during the warmer months. The hole under the outdoor toilet was full when they moved in, and Blakeney never did get around to relocating the little building. You have to give him some credit though, he did dig a second hole at the edge of the clearing and put a short 2x12 plank over top of it for easy squatting. However, with the mosquitoes and blackflies so thick, it soon became apparent that they would never be able to use the hole without sitting in a pail of insect repellent first. So a blanket was tacked across one corner of the kid's bedroom so they could do the job in a pot, then run out and dump it into the hole.

After Dorothy was born in 1918 and immediately developed rickets from a lack of food as simple as milk, eggs, fish, and berries, all of which were cheap and readily available, Blakeney decided to get a job in town. Perry had already packed up and gone to work as a clerk for the Temiskaming and Northern Ontario railway.

Dad quit school that spring, without completing grade seven, and spent most of the summer and fall, fishing, hunting, and picking berries with Mr. Trembley, an old man who lived near the Station. He stayed home all winter, hunting grouse, snaring rabbits, cutting and hauling wood, and wahtever else he could to help his mother with the burden of caring for his sufferring baby sister and his ten-year-old brother. But when the weather finally turned nice in the spring, he left home and got a job as a water-boy on a Bridge and Building gang with the T&NO.

Blakeney had quit coming home regularly during the winter because the snow on the trail made frequent visits too difficult. The best he could do was send a little money to the Widdifield store so Herman could buy food enough for survival.

But survival was getting more and more difficult for Lucy every day. With Herman gone, she only had Gordon to depend on, Fortunately, he had become a very capable young man and worked tirelessly cutting wood for the winter ahead, carrying water, fishing for trout, picking berries, and fetching groceries from the store.

As she watched Gordon's unflagging efforts, the rather unjust resentment she felt toward Herman grew deeper. She felt that Herman had abandoned them. Although Perry had done the same thing years earlier, she harbored no grudge against him because he sent her a bit of money once in a while. She Felt that Herman should send some money to her too, even though he made barely enough money as a water-boy to pay for his room and board, and buy boots and gloves for work.

Living alone with only Gordon to lean on, the bond between her and her youngest son grew steadily stronger as their situation became more and more perilous. It was this special feeling for Gordon that made Herman jealous and antagonistic toward his brother, and eventually resulted his the theft of his brother's bride-to-be.

With very money coming from Blakeney, Lucy didn't even have the few essentials to ease Dorothy's agony from the terrible calcium deficiency disease that caused her bones to break whenever she tried to stand. Nor could she give Gordon anything more than bread and molasses for his school lunch. When she did, he'd throw it off the bridge over the North River on the way to school, because he didn't want the other children to see him eating molasses sandwiches.

He didn't go to school very often anyway. It was a two-mile walk, mostly along a deer trail. In the winter it was and the snow was too deep, to walk all that way there and back. December and January were definitely out because the bush trail was already too dark to see anything, by the time school got out at 4:00pm. In March and April, the melting snow made walking without snowshoes impossible. Feet sank deep into the soft, wet snow with every step. Even deer and moose were in constant danger of becoming trapped in the decaying snow drifts.

Some years, 'April showers' would make walking the trail a misery. Mud and water replaced the snow in every low spot. At times, when it was absolutely necessary to get to Widdifield Station, he had to make wide detours through the bush around those that were too deep. Even then by the time he got to the small store, his ankle-high gum rubber boots would be filled with mud and water. Going to school at those times was out of the question.

By late April, he couldn't go because of the mosquitoes and blackflies. They were so bad in the bush that many newborn fawns died within days of birth from insect bites. In order for Gordon to survive the walk to school, he'd have to carry a cannister of blood plasma to replace what he'd lose running the blood-sucking gauntlet.

They were getting to the end of their rope by the end of March, 1920. She had to get out of there. Everyone else had deserted her, so why should she continue to stay and watch her remaining two children starve to death. Food had become so scarce that she finally had to resort to eating the pig-feed left over after Blakeney slaughtered their only animal two years earlier. Mr. Trembley, who dad had befriended before he left home, brought her trout whenever he could catch any. In the winter months, whenever he could make it into her place, he'd brought her rabbits that he snared and some potatoes. But he couldn't snare rabbit now that the snow had gone, and the river was still too high and muddy to catch fish.

In the face of her predicament she sent Gordon out to

the small enclosure on the off chance that the pig-feed pellets had become moldy and might still be edible. To his surpprise, the 40-pound bag was still half-full of crisp, clean granules. Blakeney had rolled the top of the bag tightly to remove all air and sealed it with masking tape. It didn't look too appetizing, but it was just corn, oats, soybeans and whey, with a bit of fish meal and animal fat, all of which people eat every day. It was fish meal and fat that gave it the pig-feed smell.

The best she could do to mask the smell was make soup seasoned with whatever spices she could find in her barren cupboards. They were hungry enough that it tasted rather good, and they ate little else for three weeks until the trail became dry enough to get to the Station.

It was early April, and Mr. Trembley had borrowed an old car from a neighbor to help her move to town. He parked it at the North River bridge and walked in to the house.

"It's a dang good job, I didn't try to drive in," he told Lucy. That trail isn't fit for a mule."

They strapped Dorothy onto an old, heavy oak luge made for hauling wood and rocks, that had belonged to one of the previous property owners. They decided to carry the two suitcases that held everything she had left of value: a photograph album, a few trinkets, and what little clothing they had that was still any good. Putting it on the sled with Dorothy would be too dangerous. If they shifted for some reason, they could hurt the girl.

The the trip to the car was a nightmare. The old luge was made to be pulled by a horse, not a woman, and old man and a boy. With Dorothy's 30 pounds on top of the 60 pound weight of the sled itself, it wouldn't budge without the combined effort of all three of them pulling and pushing. Then, when it's wide iron runners finally broke free, the sudden release of invariably sent one of two of them sprawing in the dirt.

Fortunately, the terrain was relatively flat, but even the slightest inclines meant a lot of extra work. When the trail sloped uphill, whoever was carrying the two suitcases had to leave them and help get the luge to the top, then go back and struggle with the baggage.

At one point the downhill slant was steep enough that the sled started going too fast. Gordon was hanging onto the back of it, trying to slow it down and guide it over the rocks zand gravel while Lucy and Mr. Trembley trudged along behind the rest of the stuff. Suddenly one of the runners ran over the top of a buried boulder and swung the vehicle sideways into a rut.

The sudden change in direction caused Gordon to lose his grip and he tumbled to the ground. Freed from its only restraint, the sled accelerated and careened toward the side of the trail. Dorothy screamed in terror as she was thrown violently from side to side as the runners took turns bumping over the rocks on the side of the trail.

Lucy was closest to the sled and dropped the bag she carried the instant she saw Gordon fall, and began chasing after the runaway conveyance.

"Dorothy," she screamed. "Hang on. I'm coming. I'll help you." If that thing turned over, she knew that Dorothy would be killed. She was too delicate to survive such an ordeal.

Then just when it seemed she couldn't catch up, the trail flattened and the luge slowed. It gradually came to a stop in the grass as the trail started up a gentle upward slope. Dorothy was still screaming, unaware in her fright that the wild ride was over. She grabbed at Lucy frantically when she felt her mother undoing the straps that bound her to the sled. Their tears mingled as Lucy pressed her little girl's cheek tightly against her own.

Gordon was limping when he and Mr. Trembley caught up to them a minute later. He had a badly bruised knee and lacerations on his hands from his fall.

"I'm OK, mom," he said when Lucy began to worry about it. "We're almost there. Let's leave the luge here. You can carry Dorothy the rest of the way now. Me and Mr. Trembley can bring everything else."

A short while later, they got to the parked car, thanking God for their deliverance. The old man unlocked the car and she put Dorothy into the back seat and was covering her with the blanket Grodon had brought from the luge when Mr. Trembley cursed loudly.

"Dirty dying old Dora!" he yelled. "The God damned tire is flat."

"I'll help you Mr. Trembley," Gordon volunteered, although he had never changed a tie in his life. In fact, he had only ever seen a couple of cars up close before. "What should I do?"

"First we have to take the spare off the back," Mr. Trembley answered. The boy's quick offer of help had calmed him down a bit. "There's a tire wrench under the front seat. I'll get the jack our of the back."

Twenty minutes later, after changing the tire, they were on their way to town. The two children thoroughly enjoyed their first car ride. Lucy wasn't so thrilled. By the way Mr. Trembley was gripping the wheel and jerking it back and forth, it seemed like he hadn't much driving experience and she worried that he might go off the road at any minute.

Aside from her worry though, the trip was uneventful. It was only after getting to town and making a few inquiries, that her world completely collapsed. Instead of a joyful reunion with Blakeney, she found that he had been living with another woman for a long time. Instead of being unemployed and unable to send her much money, as he claimed, he had been working more or less steadily ever since he came to town two years ago.

Hurt and angry, with no place to stay or food to eat, she asked Mr. Trembley to let her and the children off at the Baptist Church.

"I better wait for you," the old man said. "Maybe there's nobody there. Or maybe they won't be able to help you. What will you do then?"

'No," she told him. "You go on home. It's getting late and you don't want to drive that car after dark. It's too dangerous out there all alone. We are going to stay here no matter what. Somebody will help us. This is God's house."

She held his hand a moment and said goodbye.

Inside the church, the rectory was warm and richly appointed. Lucy sat Dorothy on the red wool carpet and gave her a small plush doll she found in the toy box under a small child's table then looked around for some way to announce her presence there. There didn't seem to a bell or anything, so she knocked on the door she thought might lead to the minister's living quarters. After a minute without any answer, she sat down in the wine-colored leather chair next to the one Gordon was sitting in. She took his hand.

"You are my precious darling," she told him. "I don't know what I could have done all these years without your help. I love you more than anything else in the world. Don't ever forget that."

"I love you too mom," he said. And they sat quietly, each thinking of the terrible hardships the other had endured over the past few years for absolutely nothing.

They were still holding hands when Glen Doyle, the minister, arrived fifteen or twenty minutes later.

Even after all she had been through, Lucy was a beautiful woman. At 51, she was tall and slender, with firm, full breasts, dark hair, and attractive features. Now, seated on the high-back chair holding hands with her 14-year-old son, she had a regal look that belied her shabby dress and coat.

Doyle liked her at once, and after hearing her story, was determined to do everything in his power to help her.

"How could you endure that situation for so long?" the minister asked gently. "There are so many good men who would cherish you and provide well for you and your lovely children!"

"I really believed Blakeney was doing his best to find work and provide for us," she replied, looking at her little girl on the floor. "I can see now that I was very naive. I'm only sorry that my children had to suffer so much. Now I have to do something to atone for my foolishness."

"Well let me see what I can do," he said. "I think I can find a place for you to live temporarily and I am sure we can help with medical treatment and a 'walker' for Dorothy."

"As for this young man," he continued, nodding at Gordon, "Vera, my wife, will find his some nice clothes and get him started in school again."

He got up from the chair he'd pulled up in front of them when he arrived, and moved it against the wall. "Please excuse me for a moment while I tell Vera we will be having guests for dinner."

So began his mother's ascent into upper middle-class life in North Bay. By the time dad arrived at her home that June day in 29, she had divorced Blakeney and married a highly-paid CPR engineer named Josh Gray.

Josh was an Irishman and a dedicated Orangeman with a Royal Arch Purple degree -- the highest in the fellowship. He was also an ardent small game hunter, as attested to by the grouse, pheasants, and rabbits that seemed to be forever hanging -- for 'curing' -- along the walls above the wooden stairs that led down into the basement of his home. Even though Lucy could never really warm up to my dad, Josh liked him and they had often hunted and fished together before he and Joe Ranger went to the States in 1925.

Now Lucy opened the door and greeted him cordially. "Herman," she exclaimed. "How handsome you are. It is so good to see you after all this time."

"I'm sure," he thought as he took her hand and kissed her cheek.

He said, however, "It's good to see you too mother. You are still as lovely as ever."

She stepped aside and motioned for him to come in.

"Gordon's wedding is in two days at the Baptist church, so I invited him and Ruth for breakfast with us," she said proudly. "I know you are going to love her. She is so nice."

Behind her, he saw the two of them were standing hand-in-hand in the hallway. "Wow," he said to himself "She's right. I love her already."

He put out his hand to Gordon and pulled his brother

close. "It's nice to see you, little brother," Herman said. Then, seeing the flicker of annoyance on Grodon's face, added, "but maybe I shouldn't call you 'little' any more. You've grown some since I saw you last."

He nodded toward Ruth. "And, I see you've caught yourself a real beauty!"

Gordon beamed. "I know. I was hoping you'd be jealous. Say hello to Ruth."

"Hello Ruth," He said, and smiled. When he put out his hand, she took it and placed her other hand on top of his and pressed it warmly.

"I'm so glad to meet you, too" she said and took a tiny step forward, tilting her cheek toward him for a kiss. He bent a kissed her lightly, then withdrew his hand and grasped Gordon's shoulder.

"Well Gordon, you got your wish," he declared. "I am very, very jealous!"

Gordon ginned happily. Unaware that Herman and Ruth would slip out of his life that night and leave him standing alone, heart-broken and humiliated virtually in front of the church.

No one had any idea where they went, or why, until Dorothy got a letter from Herman five months later, telling her that he was sorry for what he had done, but he and Ruth were now happily married in Tonnawanda, and Ruth was pregnant (with me). He hoped that everyone would eventually forgive him and that Gordon would find another girl as wonderful as the one he stolen from him.

The whole thing worked out very well for me, because I emerged into daylight on August 3rd, 1930, as a full-fledged U.S.

Citizen, and blessed with parents who truly loved each other.

I can't remember much about that first year in New York state. All I know is what I learned and deduced while writing this book. There is one thing though. My mother always liked to accuse dad of using me to attract young ladies by sitting with me on his knee on the front steps of our apartment building. He was handsome enough to attract women without any help from me, but he confessed that I gave them an excuse to say hello and other things like: "Isn't he just the most adorable baby. Is he yours, or are you just baby-sitting?"

According to mom, he encouraged some of the better looking ones to stay awhile and hold me. I must have enjoyed it because I still like the attention of pretty strangers. But the flirting, like all good things, came to an end, and we moved back to North Bay suddenly the following spring before dad had a chance to resume his warm weather 'bird calling' activities.

Why they left Tonnawanda was one thing, but to move back to North Bay, and face the vitriol and disdain of angry relatives and friends, is beyond all reason. Anyway, there we were in 1931, back in town for good.

Gordon rebounded by marrying Jean Carmichael, a truly wonderful girl. She was good looking, although not so beautiful as my mother. As far as Gordon was concerned, he always seemed like a bit of a wimp and I bless my lucky stars that he wasn't my father. In spite of that, I liked him when I got to know him better, but I could never picture him as the boy who'd been so brave and strong during his days with his mother in Widdifield.

I think he forgave my father and mother for their betrayal, because he always seemed quite friendly with my father. Although I don't know how long it took him to get to that point because I can't remember anything about him until my early teens.

Grandma, however, never got over what she believed to be my parents' act of unforgivable treachery. Like God, she thought the punishment for such a crime should apply to them *and* their offspring.

One time when she was baking apples pies for dinner, Grandma let me eat the apple peelings and I got a stomach ache on the way home. When mom asked what I ate at Grandma Gray's house I told her that she had let me eat the apple peelings.

"What color were they?" She asked.

"They were green."

"Did she give you any apple slices? Or any Pie?"

When I said she didn't, mom seemed to get angry, but didn't ask any more questions. Years later she admitted that she believed Grandma Gray had been making green (as in unripe) apple pie and had deliberately given me the peelings so I would suffer stomach pains.

"She couldn't very well administer the death penalty, as God might have wanted," mom told me, "but she could make me suffer a little."

Grandma Gray remained bitter to the very end -- even though Gordon himself seemed to have put the whole thing behind him. When she died in 1938, a couple of years after the death of her husband Josh, she left a house, a couple of additional city lots, a near-new car, and other valuables, to my two uncles; Gordon and Perry. Dorothy got cash, a car, and a house.

Dad, who really needed help at the time, got nothing but a leather belt, some Orangeman's robes, and a couple of other worthless trinkets that had belonged to her husband.

I remember standing with Dad and Mom in the living room of Grandma's home after the funeral and the reading of the will. It was the only time I ever saw him cry – not for her passing or for not leaving him anything in her will, but because she had died still hating him.

You have to feel sorry for her too, taking that kind of bitterness to the grave.

Chapter Two

GETAWAY

When we left Tonnawanda, N.Y. in 1931, the rumble seat of our 1929 Buick Roadster was crammed full of stylish suits, dresses, and considerable cash (stored safely out of the reach of Customs officers). Two suitcases full of shirts and miscellaneous other clothing were strapped onto the baggage rack by the rear bumper.

Dad drove, mom sat beside him, and I laid comfortably in her lap sucking on a pacifier. I was only a year old and wasn't the least bit interested in the scenery. I didn't even notice Niagara Falls when we passed by. In fact, I had no idea where we were going. Maybe I would have taken more of an interest if I hadn't been so young. I certainly would have asked why the heck we were headed to North Bay where dad's family would be anything but happy to see him again.

Mom wasn't worried about her family though. None of the Pringles except grandma had ever met Gordon, and then only very briefly and she wasn't particularly pleased with her daughter's choice for a husband. She thought his handshake was too limp; "almost womanish" she said. The rest of the family were only slightly annoyed that mom had left town without even saying goodbye.

All mom was thinking about now though, was how impressed everybody would be with dad and our beautiful new – well, almost new – Buick roadster.

By everybody she was thinking about her three brothers Earl, Clifford, and Glen. The car wouldn't impress grandpa Albert too much. He didn't care what anybody else owned. As far as he was concerned, if it didn't belong to him, it didn't exist. Besides, his only real interest was painting, and when he wasn't painting pictures, he was painting houses.

I guess paint was in the family genes. Uncle Earl was a painter too. In 1939 he went to Buffalo (where we just came from) and made a lot of money painting apartments in the new Willert Park low-income project. Clifford joined him for a while, but something that Hitler did made him mad and he returned to Canada to join the Canadian Army tank corps.

So, after clearing customs, and driving for ten hours up the two lane Trans-Canada highway to North Bay, we went directly to the Pringle house on Harriet Street, in the west end of town. It was about as far away from dad's mother, who lived in the extreme east end, as you could get. He said that the distance might keep his mother and Gordon from beating up his car with baseball bats. The car had cost more than $800.

Harriet Street was only one block long at the time, and only 200 meters from the north shore of Lake Nippising. A shallow ditch was all that separated the street from the Canadian Pacific Railway tracks that paralleled the street in an east/west direction. Passing trains were very disturbing at night, although you eventually got used to them.

The real problem with the trains, was the coal dust they belched from their smoke stacks. It meant that train schedules had to carefully checked before any laundry could be hung out to dry, else everything would come in black with coal dust.

To make matters worse, another railroad, the Canadian National Railway, cut through town only two blocks to the north, generating even more coal dust to coat homes, cars, and clothes. Like two jealous brothers, each afraid the other might outdo the other, the two railways raced each other clear across the country, from the Atlantic to the Pacific oceans.

By the time we parked in front of Grandma Pringle's house, mom had already prepared dad for the sight of her mother's disfigured face. She said that grandma Pringle had been a very nice-looking woman, with a good future as a schoolteacher in Warsaw, N.Y. until she suffered an epileptic fit and fell face down on the red-hot stove while she was cooking dinner one evening.

Her husband heard her groan and rushed into the kitchen and pulled her off the stove onto the floor. The left side her face and nose was burned black, as was her left arm, but Albert didn't notice. As his wife slid to the floor, he passed out from shock and fell down across her. The two of them lay there, face-down and unconscious, until son Clifford arrived on the scene a few minutes later and found them that way.

Clifford thought they had been murdered and stumbled into the living room, also in shock, to phone the police and report the crime. By the time he got back to the kitchen, Albert was sitting beside Gertie's prone body, trying to turn her over. He was moaning "Gertie, Gertie," over and over.

"What happened Pa?" Clifford asked, as he reached down to help turn her. But Albert had begun to sob when he saw his wife's badly burned face and arms and couldn't answer.

Horrified, Clifford slumped down beside his father and clung to him. They sat together crying and rocking slowly back and forth until what seemed like the entire county police force arrived with drawn guns a few minutes later.

When the officers saw Gertie's massive burns and singed

clothing, and the two men crying in each other's arms, it was instantly apparent that although they had a tragedy on their hands, it was no crime scene. They holstered their guns and gently helped the men to their feet and into the living room. The ambulance attendants, who had arrived with them, took over and quickly strapped Gertie onto a stretcher, applying temporary first aid as they whisked her away.

She survived the ordeal but her face was so badly disfigured she resembled a creature from the movie 'Night of the Living Dead'. Her psyche may have been just as deeply scarred, because all my memories are of a mean, heartless religious fanatic.

However, it's quite likely that what I perceived as malice and viciousness was the result of loneliness and insecurity after Albert's death in the winter of 1935/36.

Albert made his living as a house painter and paperhanger, and didn't leave her much in the way of insurance or assets. I was still too young to remember anything about him except that he was a talented wooden toymaker and made wooden 'hobby horses' for my brother Clyde and I for Christmas, 1935, just before he died. He was also a fine artist, painting wildlife scenes on velvet. I had one of two moose with their horns locked in mortal combat. It disappeared during my time in the Canadian Air Force.

As I mentioned in the introduction, everybody has different memories and impressions of the same situation. My sisters, Jeri and Charlotte, always loved Grandma Pringle and thought she very kind. Clyde's experiences with her were similar to mine.

The most vivid memory I have of Grandma Pringle is being imprisoned by her on the day my sister Charlotte was born at home on July 20, 1934.

We were then living in a small house next to her and she had come over to help my mother through the home-birthing ordeal.

Mom was laying on a makeshift bed in our living room, waiting for the doctor to arrive and help deliver the baby.

This black and white photo of Grandma Pringle was taken from her good side and except for the missing right nostril, doesn't reveal the full extent of the terrible discoloration and scarring on the right side of her face.

    I guess Grandma thought I might get in the way, so she took me out to a small unfinished shed in the back yard and told me to stay there until the doctor left. The little building had no floor, only bare ribs of 2x4 stringers waiting for finishing boards that never came. The space below them was littered with empty cans, bottles, and who knows what else. I was terrified and wailed loudly as Grandma left.

    A long time afterward, she came back and took me into the house. The doctor had gone and mom was holding something that I thought was one of my sister Jeri's dolls, wrapped in a small blanket.

I don't know how accurate the memory is. I was only four. But one thing is certain. I feared and hated her ever after for making me stay alone in that shed.

Fortunately, the trauma I went through that day had no effect on Charlotte entry into the world. She was born naturally without causing any undue suffering to her mother. What *did* send her life askew, was the visit a few days later of my mother's friend Irene Filiatreau. Irene had a very pronounced lisp that made it difficult for her to sound 'S' words, and it was this handicap that was responsible for a heavy burden that Charlotte was to bear for almost four decades.

Maybe if there hadn't been such a large group of neighbors fussing and cooing over Charlotte when Irene arrived, her twist of the tongue that day would have passed unnoticed. As it was, when the baby grasped her finger tightly and wouldn't let go, Irene said tenderly, "Isn't she tweet!" everybody thought it was so cute they all started referring to Charlotte as 'Tweety' Smith. The name stuck. From that moment until she was in her late thirties, Charlotte was known as Tweet.

From the very start, Charlotte disliked the name but didn't start demanding that she be called by her real name, until Bazeny Cash popularized the song 'A Boy Named Sue'.

"I suffered just as much from being called Tweet as Bazeny did with the name Sue," she told me. "I decided right then not to put up with it any more."

For awhile everyone had difficulty with the 'new' name, but eventually it became natural. Just when it did though, after 10 years or so, she decided that 'Charlotte' was a bit too long and switched to Char. I'm still confused about what I should call her.

According to mom, Grandma Pringle greeted us very warmly when we arrived back in the Bay from Tonnawanda. When she answered mom's knock on the door though, she was bent over holding onto the collar of a big brown hound dog, trying to hold it back.

"Get back in the house, " she snarled. Then, looking up, she smiled broadly and exclaimed, "Mercy me! It's you Ruth! We were wondering if we were ever going to see you again. I am so happy to you."

"I'd like to hug you, dear," she said with surprise still in her voice, "but I'll have to get this fool dog back into the house first."

"Get back, Samson," she scolded, turning her attention to the dog.

Mom watched with amusement as her mother struggled to push the wriggling dog back into the house. She succeeded in the end and shut the door behind the wagging tail.

They embraced and said how much they missed each other. "We just got into town and wanted to see you and dad before we checked into a hotel for the night," mom told her.

"Well ," her mother answered, still breathless from excitement – and her tussle with the dog. "Your father will certainly be happy to see you. We have been so worried about you."

Mom turned and took me from dad's arms, and held me up for her to see. "Meet your new grandson, momma. His name is Calvin."

"Glory be!" her mother cried. "He's a big one, isn't he? How old is he?"

"He'll be one next month, August 3rd."

"Here. Let me hold him." Grandma demanded.

Then as if she hadn't noticed dad before, she smiled and addressed him. "I suppose you are the father! Herman isn't it? We heard all about you. Welcome home."

Before dad could reply, the door opened a crack and a man's voice asked, "Who's here, Gertie?"

"You'll be surprised, Albert," she responded. "It's a little baby boy here to visit us."

"What are you talking about?" the voice was soft, but impatient. "Who's here?"

"I'm talking about your new grandson, that's what. Keep that dog back and get on out here. You can see for yourself."

Albert squeezed through the doorway, pushing Samson back with one hand. He was as tall as dad, but very thin and wiry. He smiled with pleasure when he saw mom.

"Well I'll be danged, if it isn't Ruth. What's this about a baby?"

"Take a look," grandma turned so he could see me in her arms. "Isn't he precious?" she asked.

He reached out and put his finger in my hand. I grabbed it just as mom stepped over beside him and put one arm around his neck.

"Give me a kiss, old man," she told him, "and pay me some attention. That child is always upstaging me."

He turned his head and bent to kiss her nose.

"There you go. That's all you get for running away like you did."

Then, seeing my dad watching him, he stepped forward and stuck out his hand. "I guess you're Herman. I'm Albert, her father. You two married now?"

Page 34

Dad said yes, they were, and they shook hands vigorously.

Albert nodded his head. "Welcome Herman," he said. "Come on in. Ain't no sense standing out here. We don't drink alcohol, but Gertie will make us some tea – if she's got a mind to."

The first thing you noticed when entering their house was the black iron wood stove that stood in the center of the room, about 10 feet out from the far wall. It's antique appearance set the theme for the whole room. All the furnishings were the same: rich but old. There was an assortment of small tables and footstools scattered randomly among easy chairs and two sofas. A Persian-style carpet covered most of the pine-plank floor.

"This is really a very nice room," dad commented as he and mom sat down on a sofa close to the matching easy chair that grandpa had already plopped himself into. "I like the wallpaper very much."

Grandma, who was still carrying me, walked over to grandpa. "He papered it himself," she told dad as she held me out to her husband. "He's the best interior decorator in North Bay."

"Well, don't just sit there like a lump," she ordered. "Hold this child while I go make the tea."

When she turned and started for the kitchen, dad told grandpa that we were hoping to rent "something nice like this place" as soon as possible so we wouldn't go broke paying hotel bills.

Grandma turned and stared at him. "You mean you intend to stay in North Bay?" she asked. "There's no work here. What made you decide to leave Buffalo, or wherever you were living, and come back here? It looks like you were doing pretty down there."

"Well we have a family now, and Ruth didn't think the big city was any place to raise children. Besides, there's too much crime down there!"

He didn't mention that he himself had actually been working for a mob-owned business and had left just in time to avoid being executed gangland style. According to his friend, Joe Ranger, the newspapers ran a story about a couple of mafia hitmen breaking down the door of our empty Tonnawanda apartment and shooting up the place. just three hours after we'd left, intending massacre all three of them. Joe also left town suddenly.

"I guess that's right. Nobody can argue about that," his mother-in-law agreed. "Big cities are Godless places."

Instead of questioning him further, she asked, "would you like a piece of fresh strawberry shortcake? I picked the berries myself yesterday. I know Albert wants some."

"Thank you. Yes," he answered.

Mom followed her into the kitchen to mash up some strawberries and milk for me.

"Did you see those two big houses on the corner when you turned onto our street?" grandpa asked when they'd gone. "The one on this side is up for rent by Patton and Kennedy Real Estate. You should drop in and see them."

"That's a good tip. It so happens that David Kennedy Junior is a good friend of mine. I met him when I was a bouncer at the St. Regis. They had offices there."

"Still do," grandpa told him. "I hope you can work something out with him. It'd be good to have you living close by."

The next day, dad met Mr.Kennedy and signed a lease on the Harriet St. house, paying the first month's rent in cash.

I have experienced many coincidences in my life, but none

more strange than moving into that house. The man next door was named Smith. *Gordon* Smith. Not only that, he had a son named Calvin who was born in August 1930, the same month and year as I was. How strange is that? Five years later, we were both in grade one at King George Elementary school. By that time though, everyone called him "Caggy"

Caggy's dad had a reputation for never telling the truth. "That man is the world's biggest liar," David Kennedy told dad. "He lies about everything. He can't even give his right name on a loan application."

"His wife, Grace, is a very nice lady," he added, "but all she knows is what he tells her. So it's hard to believe her either. If she tells you anything, ask her how she knows. If she says Gordon told her, forget it. He doesn't tell her the truth either."

We bought mostly all of our furniture from the second-hand stores on Oak Street over the next day or two. With the depression in full swing, good used stuff was dirt cheap. We moved into our new fully-furnished home four days after we arrived in town.

Chapter Three
THE NIGGER

Being locked in a shed full of empty bottles and cans is bad enough, but being chased home by a large black wolf can haunt your dreams forever. Even now, I am sometimes revisited by such an animal.

Clyde and I, aged four and five, were playing near the end of Harriet street at Timmins, where it ended and continued across the CPR tracks as a footpath lelading to Gorman Street and the lake. The path went down through a ditch, then up and over the tracks.

Suddenly, a big black animal with shining red eyes appeared on the tracks. It stood staring at us with shining red eyes. Then it hurtled down the path towards us. I screamed "wolf" and we both ran for home as fast as our little legs would carry us, with the wolf hot on our heels.

Ok. Wolves aren't black, and their eyes aren't red. I'm just telling you what I saw. This one was definitely black and it's eye were blazing red. I'll admit I have often thought the animal might have been a black lab, and that it might not have actually chased us, because we never looked back. If that was the case though, why would I have all these nightmares about it?

Another memory I have is of the slave-master in Grandma Pringle's kitchen. I recall that she had a ten gallon crock covered by a wooden cutting board sitting on the floor beside a side entrance door and a walk-in pantry where she stored Nabisco shredded wheat. A cooking stove sat against the wall opposite the kitchen entrance door, and in the corner beside it, sat the machine that tortured her three days out of every week – her washing machine. With a crank handle on top to turn a pair of paddles in a water-filled tank, and another on the side to force wet clothing through of a pair of rubber rollers, it treated her as if she was a little donkey trudging around in circles grinding corn.

Grandma wasn't the only slave in that era. Every woman was tied to the mind-numbing drudgery of the weekly wash. Every woman that is, except the upper-class gals who had expensive electric motor-driven machines and/or servants. Grandma's machine was a step above the scrub boards that most women had to use to get the dirt out of the household washables – every Monday, come rain or shine.

Whatever method they used, scrub board or hand-cranked machine, unless the home had running hot water, which wasn't available to those on the city's outskirts, water had to be carried from the cold-water tap to a boiler on the wood stove, then carried again to the washing machine or tub.

In grandma's case, the soiled clothing had to be agitated by means of a pair of metal fins rotated with a crank handle on the machine's lid. The woman with a scrub board had to rub each garment separately on the rough board, which was always rather hard on her knuckles.

When the clothes were clean enough, they were again hand cranked – this time through the rubber rollers into a tub of clean water beside the machine and the soap rinsed out – by hand. After rinsing, they had to be cranked back through the rollers again. The other woman was forced to wring the water out by twisting the garments by hand – an exercise that body builders use to build Schwarzenegger-sized muscles.

So now that the clothes were washed, rinsed, and wrung out, the housewife was all done. Right? Not on your life. It still had to be carried outside and pinned onto a clothesline strung between the house and a pole on the far end of the garden to dry. After a few of hours, or longer, depending on the weather, they were unpinned and carried inside to be sorted, ironed, folded, and put away the following day, usually on Tuesday. Anything with missing buttons, holes, or tears, was set aside for mending on Wednesday. If it rained while the wash was still on the line, the damp clothes had to be hurriedly brought indoors, then hung out again when the skies cleared.

With all of the coal-fired trains passing so close to our house on Harriet Street – and Timmins Street later on – white clothes, sheets, and pillow cases, tended to have a distinct grayish, sometimes blackish, tinge. Coal dust has that effect, as I learned, much to my chagrin, during my first month as a painter on the T&NO railway in 1945.

I'd seen lots of freight trains passing our Timmins Street home, but had never been on one prior to joining the railway paint crew. Now here I was actually living in a real box car on a siding in Rouyn, Quebec. We had just finished painting the outsides of various railroad sheds and storage houses, and the four cars we lived and ate in had been hooked up to a freight train that was about to move us to Kirkland Lake.

It was a hot summer's day and the five men in our crew were lying shirtless on their bunks waiting for the move. I was standing outside on the platform at the back of the car. An iron ladder beside the door led up to the roof and I was curious. So, with nothing better to do, I climbed up to have a look

There was a two-foot wide wooden walkway running down center of the car. "Say," I thought. "This would be a great place to ride. I could stretch out in the sun and get tanned, while enjoying the breeze from the moving train." Excited, I climbed back down and went inside. As I took off my my shirt, I told Emmet Kennedy, the man who had the bunk opposite me, that I was going to ride on top for a while and get tanned.

"I wouldn't do that if I were you," he said. "that's pretty dangerous."

"I'll be careful," I answered. "I'm just going to lay right there by the ladder."

"Well, it's your neck, sonny," he conceded, and turned his back. I went outside and climbed the ladder again.

"That guy is stupid," I thought as I reclined on the wooden walkway waiting for the train to start moving. "There's no way I can get hurt up here. I can't very well fall off."

The light breeze blowing across the top of the car felt good. The engine at the head of the train was idling and its

Page 42

smoke drifted lazily away toward the town.

Suddenly, the train made a violent leap forward as the couplings between the cars locked together. I was startled and grabbed the edges of the walkway to keep from falling off. But then the train began to move smoothly forward and I relaxed.

"That was nothing," I said to myself. "What the heck was old Emmet talking about? Dangerous my eye!"

In fact it was dangerous – my eye. The coal dust from the engine's smoke stack was drifting back to me now and I had to squint to keep it out of my eyes. It felt like being in a wind storm on the desert, except the blowing sand was tiny bits of coal. I closed my eyes and lay my head down on the wood.

As the train began to gain speed, and the intensity of the coal dust hitting my bare shoulders increased. It didn't bother me too much at first so I lay there trying to ignore it. Soon however, the wind began to feel more like sandpaper than blowing air. I could stand it no longer and slid backwards onto the ladder and climbed down.

When I opened the car door and walked inside the bunk car I was greeted with howls of laughter.

"Where'd that Nigger come from?" somebody asked.

"Man, that's the deepest tan I ever saw," hollered another.

I was shocked when I looked in the mirror. My upper body was pitch black and my hair was thick with coal dust. Underneath it all, my skin looked and felt as if I had been sunburned. Worst of all, I was thoroughly humiliated.

Clothes hanging on a line in the back yard are rarely exposed to such a large amount of coal dust so forcefully administered. Nevertheless, a stiff breeze can sometimes prove equally devastating to the woman doing the wash. Having to rewash and dry all those clothes would be enough make a saint want to plant a bomb on the tracks.

Household chores were so tedious and time consuming in those days that a six day routine had been established and practiced in almost every home in America. It was even taught by first grade teachers to the classes in the form of a poem. The lines concerning the chores for Thursday, Friday, and Saturday, describe housecleaning and other labor intensive work aren't relevant to clothes washing, The first three lines are:

> *Monday we wash,*
> *Tuesday we iron,*
> *Wednesday we mend and sew.*

Chapter Four

SINGING TO THE BEARS

With all the housework women had to do, you have to wonder why they wanted more and more babies. All that does is increase their workload. Mom had enough to do with three kids, but after Charlotte was born, it got even harder. The baby had to be fed, rocked, burped, changed, and soothed. Bottles had to be boiled and rinsed. Baby shirts had to be changed after every feeding. Cloth diapers had to be changed, rinsed out, soaked, boiled, and washed by hand. Disposable diapers wouldn't be available in the late 1940s. Even then, they wouldn't come into widespread use until the '70s.

That was the reason mom wasn't able to go picking berries with dad in August the year Charlotte was born. I was happy though, because he took me instead.

In late summer, much of Northern Ontario's forests literally turn blue with big, sweet blueberries; particularly in places that had been burned out in the previous few years. My dad knew of just such a place in the bush 10 miles east of town and decided to go picking there and take me with him. If I was out of the way it would lighten mom's workload a bit. She would only have Clyde, Jeri, and the baby to take care of. Nothing to that!

The doctor bills had piled up pretty high over the previous nine months – thanks to Charlotte -- and dad needed to make a little extra money. Picking and selling wild blueberries door to door was an easy way to do that. Well, it was for me anyway.

So early one morning he hoisted me to his shoulders, picked up two empty 11-quart baskets and walked two miles to the edge of town, where he hitched a ride to a well-hidden trailhead off of highway 17.

We had hardly started up the vague, overgrown trail when he told me there would probably be some black bears in the berry patch, fattening up for the long winter months ahead. He said we should make lots of noise to warn them we were coming so they could get away before we got there.

He didn't need to add that "bears just love to eat little boys." Even at four years old, I could figure that out for myself.

"What kind of noise should I make?" I asked.

"Well, how about we sing a loud song?" he suggested.

"I don't know any, except Three Blind Mice," I admitted.

Dad wasn't much of a singer, but he loved Poetry, especially Robert Service stuff. He had memorized most of the 'Ballads of the Yukon' poems, and recited them at every opportunity. He also made up a lot of rhymes himself. One that I hated, and that my three sons disliked just as much when I recited it to them in the mornings later, was his wake-up call:

> *Arise, arise, my bully byes.*
> *It's now the break of day.*
> *Your breakfast you must take*
> *Your axes and your saws*
> *and go out into the wild woods*
> *to the banks of the Kagaboz,*
> *Arise, arise, arise.*

After he thought about the three blind mice for a minute he said, "I got it. Lets change the blind mice into *black bears* and the farmer's wife into *a little boy*. That should scare the rascals!" He started singing and changing words until he finally had a song we both liked and we sang it over and over the rest of the way to the berry patch.

> *"Three black bears, see how they run.*
> *"They all ran after the little boy.*
> *"He cut off their tails with a sharp edged toy,*
> *"Three black Bears."*

The song was corny, but our singing must have worked. We never saw hide nor hair of a bear all day long. We did spot a large patch of blue bear-poop near a big log though. Dad pointed to it and said, "See that, son? There were bears here alright. We must have scared the poop out of them and they all ran away!"

It was a hot, sunny day and four year old boys weren't meant to labor under such conditions. So any blueberries that I picked went right into my mouth. Dad said he didn't really need any help anyway, so I spent my time exploring the rocks and bushes in the large clearing, always keeping him in sight in case a momma bear showed up.

I discovered a nest of garter snakes under a big flat rock, that scattered as soon as I touched it. I wasn't afraid of snakes of course, because we had a lot of them around our house and I had even picked one up. But I'd never seen 'wild' ones before, or any so big. A couple of these were about as long as one of my dad's yardsticks.

I wanted to see if I could catch one and searched around the rocks and bushes for quite a while before I finally found one. It wasn't very big but I wasn't going to hurt it, just tame it down a bit, then let it go. It thrashed around in my hand and stunk me up with its scent bomb, but it didn't try to bite like dad said the big ones do. Anyway, he said that the bites don't hurt all that much. Not like bees for sure!

I wondered how he knew that? He was deathly afraid of snakes, even harmless ones, and to my knowledge he had never been bitten. He had certainly never picked one up. In fact, he became almost paralyzed with fear at the sight of them. One time after we moved to the country, I dragged the tail of a little mouse over his hand while he was napping. He woke with a start thinking it was a snake and panicked, He began yelling "kill it. kill it kill it." When I showed him that it was only a mouse, he wanted me to kill it anyway. I took the little thing outside and let it go.

    All in all, the day was fun, but uneventful. After dad had the baskets filled, we headed back down the trail to the highway. We stood on the edge of the highway holding hands for more than an hour trying unsuccessfully to get a ride back to town. I was really tired by then so he picked me up and sat me on his shoulders. I guess it made a rather touching picture because the very next car stopped and drove us all the way to our door. I think the lady liked us – him.

Chapter Five

HOLY ROLLING

Dad and mom were always good to us, but not really affectionate. I don't remember either of them ever kissing us or saying they loved us. On the other hand, they never spanked us either, and seldom yelled or got really mad at us for anything. However, their dislike of any form of corporal punishment made both of my grandmothers furious.

Grandma Gray didn't come right out and say anything to them about it, but she often told me that I was spoiled rotten and that my mother "should learn how to raise kids if she was going to keep on having them."

Grandma Pringle was a religious zealot with a firm belief in the child-rearing maxim '*Spare the rod, spoil the child*". Her belief in spanking created a lot of conflict between her and my parents. Many of their frequent loud arguments were the result of her twisting our ears whenever she got the chance.

Then there was the fact that my mother wouldn't let Grandma take me to church with her on the grounds that "he's only four and wouldn't understand anyway. Besides it's too far for him to walk."

Grandma settled that last argument about being 'too far to walk', when the money that dad brought with him from Tonnawanda finally ran and we were evicted from our house on Harriet Street. She talked the Pentecostal church elders into renting us the big red-brick house they owned next to the church on McIntye Street.

Now, because we were living right next to the church, Mom had no more excuses why we shouldn't be able to go to Sunday School. Grandma began dragging me and Clyde to church with her anytime she felt like it.

I never quite got used to her behavior in church. She'd suddenly jump up and yell stuff at the preacher – things like 'praise God', 'Amen', 'Hallelujah', 'Yes Lord, come and get me' – and other things I didn't understand. Not that she was the only one that did that. People were popping up and down all the time, yelling similar things. Sometimes everybody seemed crazy!

After the sermons, the minister would take my Grandmother and the other really noisy ones into a back room for a more 'intimate relationship with Jesus'. Clyde and I would go to another room to listen to stories of Jonah, Daniel, and other bible heroes. Sometimes God was really bad, like the time He answered Elisha's prayer and sent bears down to kill 42 children for teasing him about his bald head.

When I grew older, I often heard Pentecostals referred to as 'Holy Rollers' and wonder to this day if it had anything to do with what went on in that mysterious back room. Whatever it was, it had a huge influence on Grandma's youngest son Glen. He enrolled in a Pentecostal college in 1942. When he was ordained in 1946 he married Dorothy Tunks, a fellow graduate. Their marriage was spotted with extra-marital affairs on both sides. But they still stuck it out together, apparently happily, for more than sixty years, until Glen died in 2008.

Glen had always seemed soft spoken and mild-mannered to me, until I attended one of his sermons shortly after he got his first assignment as minister of a church in Bracebridge, Ontario. Standing on a platform in front of his congregation, he jumped up and down, shook his fists, and shouted loud and long about how Hell waited for those who didn't "walk with the lamb."

"Praise God!" Dorothy echoed.

His face red, his finger jabbing and pointing, the buttons of his suit straining beneath his heaving chest, he shouted, "Turn from your sinful ways. Jesus loves all of you. Even those of you who don't deserve it."

"That's right." Dorothy screamed. "He shows compassion for human frailties,"

"Praise God," came the roar of the congregation.

"Amen." yelled Glen, "Christ came into this world because of his compassion for our slavery to sin. Although he came in the form of God, Jesus emptied himself and then took the form of a slave; being born, as he was, in the likeness of men."

"Hallelujah," cried Dorothy.

"Glory be to Jesus," chorused the crowd.

"Let us pray," Glen murmured.

"Bullshit," I groaned.

Dorothy shared the pulpit with him, but limited her performance to affirming his rants and singing a few hymns after the sermon. Glen played the saxaphone while she played the guitar and sang *"Just a little talk with Jesus"* and a few other popular Pentecostal hymns. The congregation knew them all and joined in. I didn't participate, but I have to admit that I enjoyed the show.

All in all, Glen did a great imitation of an over-the-top, revival-tent healer. I think he would have done Jimmy Swaggart proud, although, as with Swaggart's performances years later, I enjoyed the act, but thought the message was for the weak of mind.

Glen wasn't only a dynamic religious performer, he was also a great door to door salesman. In 1955, he was named Salesman of the Year by the Fuller Brush company. I guess he inherited his salesmanship – as he did his religious fervor – from

Grandma. She too, was quite successful selling stuff door-to-door in spite of her horribly scarred face and burned-off nose (or maybe because of it, and the sympathy it evoked). Through rain and snow, heat and cold, always in danger of suffering another epileptic seizure, she trudged the streets of North Bay, and still later of Toronto, ringing doorbells to sell bibles, christian calendars, cards, and wall plaques to support herself, the church, and Jesus.

Chapter Six

EARTHQUAKE

On the second day of September 1935, mom walked me to school for my first day in Kindergarten, and stayed with me for a while until I adjusted to the experience. Then she left with a promise to come back and pick me up at four. My adjustment couldn't have been complete though, because no sooner had she gone than I created a large puddle under my desk.

The teacher dried the floor, but there was nothing she could do about my pants, so I sat in them until mom got back. I recall being ashamed, but none of the children even seemed to notice.

We were still living on McIntyre Street a couple of months later when the city was visited on Halloween night by the worst earthquake ever recorded in that area. Seven hours after we returned home from Trick or Treating. Jeri (who's registered name was Geraldine, usually shortened to Gerry, but changed to Jeri in later years), and I were asleep in separate beds in "the kids room" when our brick house began to shake. Dad was working as night watchman at a local lumber yard and mom had Clyde in bed with her, while Charlotte slept in a crib alongside of them. Clyde had been plagued with some kind of dangerous illness for a year after his birth and mom was still (overly) protective of him. The only thing wrong with him that night, was that he had eaten too much Halloween candy.

Mom awoke about 1:00am thinking that the house was

falling down. The bed was bouncing, bottles and dishes were crashing, and bricks from the chimney were rolling down the roof. In a panic, she ran into our room and dragged Jeri and I out of our beds and back to her room. Charlotte was still sleeping soundly in the crib, but Clyde was now awake and crying. She put Jeri and I into bed beside him and crawled in with us, hanging on to the three of us and holding tightly onto Charlotte's crib.

By the time we had all settled down the shaking had stopped and, except for Clyde's whimpering, the night was quiet. By the time Dad got home to check on us everybody but mom was fast asleep. I don't know how long he stayed, or what he did, but he had gone back to the lumber yard by the time we kids got up in the morning. Apparently there were numerous aftershocks throughout the night, and for months afterward. It was said that some buildings shifted and many people left their homes temporarily. There were no casualties.

It remains a mystery to me how we got so many Christmas gifts that year. All I know is that mom put half of them away and doled them out to us a couple at a time for the rest of the year. My favorite was a Gene Autry cap gun made from cast white metal, which was to toys in those days, what plastic is today.

One day, I was shooting off caps on the front sidewalk because mom didn't want me firing the gun in the house. Clyde was with me, but I didn't want him to use the gun for fear he'd drop it on the cement walk and break it. White metal shatters easily and can't be repaired. Clyde already had a history of throwing tantrums and breaking things that belonged to me and I didn't trust him.

When I wouldn't let him have the gun he ran in to tell mother. She came out and took the gun from me and handed it him. Without any hesitation, he raised it above his head and slammed it down on the concrete, breaking it into pieces. Then he started crying again and mom picked him up carried him back inside, patting his back.

"There, there," she soothed, again and again. "It's Ok. Don't cry."

I was left on the sidewalk, as shattered as Gene Autry's toy gun. His behavior that day, became the pattern for almost everything he did throughout his life.

Clyde was extremely handsome and had a deceptively charmingly manner that put you off guard. Then, just as you were beginning to like him, he'd turn on you and do or say something to make you hate him again.

Chapter Seven
SERIAL KILLER

We moved into a two-story yellow wood-frame house at 272 Copeland Street in the spring of 1936 for twenty-five dollars a month. The house was owned by a widow named Granger who lived in an upscale home on Jane Street directly behind us. She seemed a little bit cold at first but turned out to be a very nice lady.

The best thing about living there for us children was the many kids our age that lived in the neighborhood around us. Dad didn't share our enthusiasm, because they were mostly French. He didn't like French people, Jews, or blacks. But we didn't see any difference, except that we could call them 'Frogs' and tease them with silly chants like "Pea soup and Bazeny cake will make a Frenchman's belly ache". They had names and chants they could reciprocate with, so we got along very well together.

When dad got into a fist fight with Mr. Turcotte next door, none of the kids, either Turcotte or Smith, took it personally and continued to play in each other's yards. I didn't know what started the fight or who won, but I often boasted teasingly to the Turcotte kids afterward that "my dad can beat your dad". They never let that brag pass without loud argument.

Our house was one block west of the CNR railway crossing on Copeland street, and a block north of them as they headed west along McIntyre street. A box-making factory between us and the tracks provided some protection from the noise and coal dust that spewed from the passing trains. But the factory itself was annoying with high pitched whine of its steam-powered rip-saws penetrating the daylight hours. The factory made light-weight wooden fruit and vegetable baskets from thin slices of pine veneer and closed down in the forties when wood was replaced by cardboard and molded fiber.

There was a small store named Lowneys three blocks east of us on McIntyre Street. It was similar to todays mom and pop convenience stores and sold everything from canned sardines to beef bologna. The bologna was only 10 cents a pound and came with a free pound of beef liver. They also carried a lot of fresh meat and groceries and a large variety of penny candies. It was only a couple of minutes walk from our house and we seemed to be constantly going there for something or other.

On my way to the store one day, I met a kid who was always picking on me at school. He was older and bigger than I was, and liked to twist my arm behind my back until I had to go down on my knees with the pain. Sometimes he'd put his foot behind mine and shove me backwards so I'd fall. That day though, he had his arms full of groceries and greeted me as if we were regular pals.

"Hi Cal," he said. "Are you going to Lowneys? My mom

gave me a nickel for going to store for her, and I bought a whole bag of candy."

"What do I care if you have candy?" I thought. "This is my chance to get even."

His arms were too full to fight back. He wouldn't drop the bags and if he took the time to set them down carefully, it would give lots of time to get away. Here was a fight I couldn't lose!

I swung a punch that connected with his nose. I don't know whether it bled, of if he dropped the groceries, or even if he tried to chase me. All I remember is him yelling; "I'll get you Monday, you coward."

Ouch! There was a way I could lose that fight after all. I had forgotten all about school in my excitement. True to his word, he did get me back, with interest, and more than once.

One time my uncle Perry gave me a quarter to get some treats at the store. As a baggageman on the T&NO railway he made very good money and twenty-five cents wasn't all that much money to him. He lived in Rouyn, Quebec, so we didn't see much of him. But been visiting the T&NO head office in North Bay for something and came up to our house to visit. He and dad got to drinking the home brew that dad made and I guess he got pretty mellow.

It turned out that my idea of a *'treat'* wasn't what he or my siblings had in mind because they were all upset when I returned with four penny candies, a loaf of bread, a can of peanut butter, a can of sardines, and a can of beans. I thought I had spent the money very wisely.As far as I was concerned, any kind of food was a treat.

About the only thing we didn't buy from Lowneys was milk and bread. Both were delivered directly to our door every morning by horse-drawn milk and bread wagons – if and when we enough money to buy tickets. Horse-drawn wagons also delivered ice, which was used in the ice-boxes to refrigerate food. Coal and wood were delivered by horse drawn sleighs in the wintertime.

All of the delivery wagons traded their wheels for heavy oak iron-clad runners during the winter months. They wouldn't have been able to operate otherwise. Snowplows were used to pile the snow along the edges of the streets, but salt wasn't in common use and the streets remained heavily packed with ice and snow from November until mid March. Like everything else, both the weather and snow removal methods have changed dramatically since then.

Kids today will never know the ecstasy of real ice cream. It was produced by the milkmen who always left milk on the doorstep very early in the morning so it would be fresh for breakfast. It was pasteurized but not homogenized in those days, so the cream always rose quickly to the top of the bottle. In freezing winter temperatures, the cream froze before the milk and because it expands when frozen, squeezed up and out the top of the bottle, lifting the cardboard bottle cap jauntily as it did. The result was a two or three inch white cylinder of pure ice-cream sticking out of the bottle neck. It made a delicious treat but was never enough for four hungry kids.

The wagon drivers did their best to keep kids off their vehicles. Everybody with skates, sleighs, or skis tried to sneak a tow on the back of their horse-drawn wagons. The horses never moved very fast, so the sleighs were easy to catch and safe to ride. At least, that's what we thought. We just couldn't see the danger. To get off, all we had to do was let go and drag our feet to stop.

That's exactly what Oscar Turcotte thought too, the winter afternoon he hitched his toboggan onto a bakery wagon. It gets dark early in December and January, and the driver didn't see him catch on. This time though, Oscar hung onto the bread sleigh longer than he should have – all the way to the railway crossing at the end of the block. Once over the tracks, the road took a sharp dip downward and, although the horse didn't speed up, Oscar's toboggan did. Unable to slow down on the sharp decline, he slid under the wagon into its undercarriage and smashed his head. I'm not sure now exactly how bad his injuries were, but they were severe enough to send him to the hospital for a while.

    I always wished that it had been Paddy Pileau that had been crushed under the wagon. Even at the age of six, that kid was in the initial stages of becoming a pathological serial killer. He enjoyed torturing – and killing – insects, birds, and animals. I don't know if he had any problems at home but there didn't seem to be. He was always laughing and didn't have any outward signs of physical abuse. He just seemed obsessed with tormenting living creatures. He loved hunting the rats that scavenged the garbage piles in the neighborhood, slashing them with his hoop stick (a wooden slat with a cross piece nailed onto it near the bottom for pushing metal barrel hoops along the sidewalk) until their insides spewed out.

    He told me once that he had tied a firecracker to a dog's tails on Halloween and lit it, and described how the dog ran around in circles trying to bite the thing off. Then one day he found a nest full of baby birds and set it on fire. When he began showing the charred remains to everyone in the block, Henri Turcotte took it away from him and gave him a nose bleed.

    On another occasion, my sister Jeri saw him tie a rope around a cat's neck and swing it around and around over his head, then smash it again and again, into the stone wall surrounding the Polangio residence on the west corner of the street. The dead animal stayed there until the smell became unbearable and someone disposed of it. Jeri was only four at the time and too young to do anything but watch in horror.

I wish I knew what become of Paddy. He disappeared from the neighborhood sometime that winter. I suppose his family probably just moved away.

Chapter Eight

POLIO

One October afternoon I started feeling sick at school just before the final bell and it was all I could do to walk the few blocks home. By the time I got there, my temperature was high, I felt faint, and my legs were stiff and hurt to bend. Mom saw instantly that something was seriously wrong so she put me to bed and phoned the doctor. I fell asleep immediately.

I woke up briefly when Doctor Bowers arrived (doctors still made house calls in those days) and gave me a shot of something in the back. I lost consciousness again and knew nothing more for two weeks. During that time no one was allowed to leave or enter the house. I had polio and a quarantine sign had been plastered on our door.

Dad, of course, couldn't go to work until I fully recovered so he spent countless hours massaging my back and neck, and bending my joints. He told me later that I was so rigid at first he could put one hand under my neck and lift me up like a board.

There were six other cases of polio in North Bay that fall and I was the only one that fully recovered. All of the other children ended up crippled. No one died.

In the spring it was Dad's turn, but he was in much more pain than I had been. One side of his back had swollen up like a balloon. He was admitted to the Civic hospital in North Bay for less than a day, while tests were done on his kidneys, and then rushed by ambulance to Toronto for an emergency kidney operation. His kidney was too badly infected to save, and it had to be removed. After a week in Toronto, he was returned to North Bay where he remained in the hospital for weeks while his back healed.

Most surgeons at the time were little more than butchers with limited knowledge and crude instruments. The one who operated on my dad's back wouldn't even be allowed to watch an operation in today's world. The healthy tissue that was sliced out of his back to get at the kidney, must have weighed five pounds. He still had a half-liter sized cavity in his back when he died 53 years later.

Worse than the operation itself was the healing process. The dressings needed to cover the wound were necessarily huge and were secured by adhesive tape that couldn't be removed with taking all of the hair and much of the skin with it. I don't know how they got the bandages off in the hospital, but no amount of soaking with water, baby oil, or alcohol did much at home. The skin wounds, secondary infections, and trauma from bandage removal resulted in frequent re-hospitalization over the following months.

During all this time we had no source of income other than a little bit of welfare money – which dad called "the pogey". Grandma Pringle helped us out a bit, but then she petitioned the city to take the kids away from mom and put us into a foster home, saying we were being neglected. The investigators rejected the petition on the grounds that it was 'frivolous'. Dad's mother didn't help us either. She didn't visit him in the hospital or at home. Nor did she ever give us a single penny, or even a loaf of bread.

I didn't really know the full extent of our need because we children were never starvation hungry and were completely unaware of how our clothing fit or looked on us. But I did know we needed money. So when one of the Polangio teenagers who lived in a big mansion-like home on the corner where Paddy had finally disposed of the cat, laid his school books and lunch money on the sidewalk in front of our house and went back home for something he had forgotten, I ran out, took the money and went into hiding in some bushes in our back yard.

It was my first felony – and one of the few that I will ever admit to in print. Fortunately, it went completely unnoticed by the victim, who returned to the scene a few minutes later, picked up his books and continued on to school. I guess the 20 cents I stole didn't mean very much to him. His father owned Deluxe Transportation and Taxi, one of the most successful businesses in town, and the boys always had the best of everything. But even that little bit of money meant bread, meat, and rolled oats to my mother, who believed me when I told her I had found it out on the road.

I did make a bit of money legitimately, working for our landlady. My mother had taken me with her one spring day when she went to ask Mrs. Granger for a rent deferment until we could arrange for help from the city. Our medical bills since we moved into the house had been astronomical, first me with polio, and then my dad with his kidney removal.

Mrs. Granger opened the door just as mom was about to press the doorbell a fourth time.

"Well, hello Mrs. Smith," she said. "I'm sorry to keep you waiting so long. I was just making tea. How are you managing down there anyway? Is your husband getting better?"

"Actually, he's suffering more from the bandages than from the operation itself," mom replied. "He's back in the hospital being treated for skin wounds from the adhesive. I think they might discontinue the bandages altogether now. I hope so anyway. The wound is almost healed."

"He has certainly gone through a lot, hasn't he?" Mrs Granger sympathized. Then she turned her attention to me.

"And how are you, Calvin? Aren't you the tough guy, fighting off that terrible polio like that? I hear a lot of children didn't fare so well."

I said I was fine and that I didn't know any of the kids who had been crippled, but that I felt sorry for them anyway.

"Well you certainly don't look any worse for wear," she said. "Anyway, come on in, both of you. We'll have some tea and cookies."

She stood aside and motioned us in, then led the way to a room with a huge polar bear rug on the floor. The bear's head faced the door and its big yellow eyes glared at us. I stopped short and backed away.

"Don't worry Calvin," Mrs Granger smiled. "he's very friendly. You can pet him if you want. Here, let me introduce you. His name is Nanuk. My husband brought him back from Alaska."

Taking my hand, she led me over to the rug.

"Why don't you sit on his back?" she invited, bending down to pet the bear's head. "Nanuk likes big boys like you."

She stood and took my mother's arm. "Come, have a seat over here while I go pour us some tea. Would Calvin like a glass of milk?"

"That would be wonderful," mother said. "It's not often we get such a nice invitation. I'm just sorry that I have to ask a favor of you in repayment for your kindness."

"Let's not discuss it until we get some cookies into Calvin's stomach," Mrs. Granger suggested. "it can't be all that serious." With that she left the room.

"It's too bad Mrs. Granger isn't my grandmother," I thought. She was really nice and smelled nice too – just like the flowers along the sidewalk into her house. Grandma Pringle smelled bad.

The two of them drank tea and chatted about things that didn't interest me. I ate home-made ginger cookies and drank a glass of milk. Then my mother made her plea.

"I know we are behind on our rent payments, Mrs. Granger," she began, "and I have applied to the city for help. But they told me they can't do anything until the end of the month. Of course, you need money like anyone else, but would it be possible for you to wait for our rent money that long?"

"My dear Mrs. Smith," the woman replied. "I'll make a deal with you. If you can convince that young man of yours – she looked pointedly at me – to dig the dandelions out of my lawn, I'll be more than happy to wait for the city to act. In fact, I know some people down there, and I might be able to speed things up for you."

Hearing that I jumped up off the bear skin.

"I'll dig the dandelions for you Mrs Granger," I said. "I'll just run home and get a shovel."

Both women smiled at my enthusiasm.

"You don't have to do that, Calvin," Mrs Granger responded. "I have everything you need in the shed out back. We'll go get it later."

"But," she added, "you didn't let me finish, dear. I was about to say that I would pay you one cent each for all the dandelion roots you dig out. That way I can be sure there won't be a single one left to ruin my nice lawn."

She said she had a few things she had to do that day, but

we could start tomorrow, "If that would be alright with your mother."

The deal was done. I went back the next morning and she showed me how to dig the roots out with a little trowel and put them into a bushel basket for counting later. After she watched me remove a few dandelions without inflicting too much damage on the surrounding grass, she went inside and left me alone; although I saw her watching me from the window from time to time.

I was proud to be working for Mrs. Granger and tried hard to do exactly as she had instructed. I knew she was happy with me too, because she came out often with lemonade, little sandwiches, and cake.

When I finished around mid-morning the next day, we counted the dandelion roots together. She paid me 62 cents, mostly pennies, which she put into a little brass pot to make it look like a pot of gold.

It really was a pot of gold to mom and I. No one else had ever done anything like that for us. But now, in a single act of kindness, our landlady eased mom's fears of eviction and, with the money she gave me, filled our cupboards with food. Sixty-two cents was more than many men made in a week in those days.

Chapter Nine

WRONG SIDE OF THE TRACKS

The worst thing about living on the wrong side of the tracks was having to attend King George Elementary School, which was located in the most prestigious residential area of town. Some of Northern Ontario's wealthiest people lived in the area around the school, including Senator Gordon, the first and only senator in North Bay's history.

The teachers were nice and the school was great. But most of the boys were from well-off families and wouldn't have anything to do with either me or Clyde, other than to bully us. We were never asked to play in any of their games.

The discrimination wasn't too pronounced when I was in grade one because we still hadn't hit rock bottom. Besides, first-graders don't tend to judge you by your address or clothing anyway. But it quickly became a problem for in grade two, once their mothers began to realize who we were. It probably wouldn't even have been so bad if it hadn't been for the clothes we wore, or – as in the case of shoes – didn't wear. While, we weren't exactly barefoot, you could always count the toes peeking out of our runners.

When the weather turned cold, our footwear changed. We had to trade our worn-out running shoes for clunky, black, ankle-high, lace-up rubber boots that cost all of $1.29 in Eaton's catalog. They were too cold to wear without thick felt insoles and two pair of heavy socks. Which meant they had to be a couple of sizes too large to accommodate all of that insulation, plus a small pair of feet. So we slogged around in boots so big and awkward we couldn't walk without dragging our feet. This alone set us apart from the well dressed kids with their cozy calf-length, leather-topped snow boots.

The only 'rich kid' that I could call friend was a chubby boy named Murray Pace. He wasn't obese, like another schoolmate, Bazeny Bazeson, who was almost too fat to walk and died at the age of 18, but he was just fat enough to be different, and therefor shunned. As he grew up, however, Murray became handsome and well built. And a celebrated obstetrician. He delivered more than 10,000 babies in 35 years of practice in the Bay and died peacefully and much loved in hospital in August 2010 at the age of 80, survived by his wife Angela and their 10 children.

Senator Gordon's mansion at 591 Copeland Street was built in 1911 within a block of King George Public School. It is now a treasured historical landmark.

With the help of the city, we were able to pay Mrs. Granger the money we owed her, but we couldn't continue paying $25 a month rent, so dad found another house two blocks further west, in North Bay's poorest low income area. The term 'Ghetto' hadn't yet been coined. If it had, the area bounded by Copeland, Timmins, McIntyre, and Nippising Streets, including both sides of the streets, would have qualified for that name. The population was a mix of low income/no income families like ourselves.

Our new house on Timmins Street cost us just $15 a month. It was small with only four rooms and no bathroom, hot water, basement, or storage areas. The word was 'cramped', but it was cheap. We moved in a few days before school started in September 1937.

In spite of a few women who entertained a lot of men, and the piles of empty Barnes Wine bottles behind most of the neighborhood homes, it was probably the safest place in town to raise children because there were very few cars and no strangers – not during daylight hours anyway.

The men that set up camp in the 'hobo jungle' at the bottom of Timmins Street, near the lake, might have been a nuisance to residents along Main Street, but they seldom came up the hill to beg food or clothing from us. The prospect of getting a handout in our neighborhood was practically zero and everybody knew it.

The only real danger was the train tracks that ran along the opposite side of McIntyre Street within 100 feet of our house. But everybody was afraid of trains and for the most part we kept well away from the tracks. Everybody 'knew' that we could be sucked into the moving boxcars if we got too close. The turbulence caused by the speeding train, plus the vertigo generated by the boxcars flashing by, seemed to pull you toward the tracks if you got within 20 feet of them. The first hint of an approaching locomotive always signaled an instant evacuation of the area close to the tracks.

Between trains, the tracks served as a shortcut to a sandy beach on the lake shore a half mile from the Girl's College. Most of our friends went there every warm day during the summer months. We walked on the rails, picked strawberries along the embankment, and shot stones at the glass insulators on the telegraph poles, along the way.

But we always remained aware of danger of getting your foot caught somehow between the rail and the wooden ties and not being able to get off the tracks in time to keep from having it amputated by an approaching train. Thus, we bent down frequently and put our ears on the rail to listen for the singing sound in the metal that signaled an approaching train while it was still miles away.

Chapter Ten

THE SUICIDE TRICK

I had occasion to apply our train track early warning system years later while hitch-hiking back to Chatham Air Force base in New Brunswick where I was stationed. Someone had let me off in an isolated stretch of highway in New Brunswick at 3:30 in the morning and, after a half hour without seeing a single car, I decided to take a nap on the side of the road. Not wanting to miss a potential ride however, I laid my head on the pavement so that I might hear any approaching vehicle in time to stand and lift my thumb.

The next I knew, a car was idling inches from my head and someone was prodding me with a stick to see if I was still living.

"Are you alright? Have you been hit?" a gruff male voice asked.

"No, no," I protested. "I fell asleep."

"You fell asleep and landed on the pavement?" the man asked. "Did you hit your head when you fell? Do you feel Ok?"

"I'm fine," I answered. "I didn't fall. I was hitch-hiking and got tired so I laid down and put my head on the pavement so I could hear when a car was coming."

"You are kidding me." he roared. "Do you mean you deliberately went to sleep with your head on the road? Were you trying to commit suicide? I came within inches of running over your f—ing skull."

I was standing by then and he whacked me with the stick.

"You idiot," he shouted. "What's that uniform you're wearing? Surely to Christ you are not in the Air Force. I don't believe it."

Three other men gathered around us, and I could see now that they had all been drinking. They were doubled over laughing at me.

"But if you listen on the pavement you can hear cars coming a long way away," I stammered.

The spectators hooted in derision and the big man slashed me again across the side of the butt.

"Where the Hell did you come up with that idea?" he asked incredulously.

"We used to do that to hear trains coming on the tracks," I replied. "It really works."

"You are really dumb," he said. "Roads are made of tar, not steel. Sound doesn't travel through tar. I should just leave you here and let some other fool run over your brainless head."

He took another swipe at me and told me to climb into the back seat.

"But don't get any more stupid ideas," he warned. "I think you're a dangerous nut and I don't want any of my friends to get hurt."

With that he too began to laugh and the four of them discussed the size of my brain and the mentality of my recruiting officers all the way to Campbelton, where we parted company.

Chapter Eleven

The Hobo Jungle

Clyde and I had been fishing in the lake and were on our way home for lunch with a couple of perch that we'd caught, when we met a hobo who, like the Pied Piper or Hamlin, played irresistable music, and we couldn't help ourselves from following him.

We'd just come up the trail to the end of Timmins Street when we saw him sitting on the ground a half-block away, near the path leading into the 'jungle'. He was playing hobo and train music on a mouth organ. They were songs we knew. Songs that dad always sang around the house; *'the wreck of the old number nine'*, *'the big rock candy mountain'*, *'Hallelujah, I'm a bum'*, and stuff like that. He was really good.

When we got too close we started edging over to the center of the road to make a wide detour around him. He quit playing and wiped his face with the red cowboy bandana he wore around his neck.

"Hello boys," he called. "Don't you like my music? It's hobo music because that's what I am now. I learned most of it riding the rails. Mostly from some of the other hobos. There's a lot of really good musicians *'riding the rods'*."

He smiled broadly and put the harmonica back in his mouth and played a few notes, twisting his head back and forth as he did, his stringy yellow hair flew back and forth across his face. When he quit playing, he looked at us and smiled.

We'd already guessed that he was a hobo from his ragged clothes and worn out shoes – just like ours – but he was different from all the old and scary bums we'd seen before. In spite of his short, straggly beard, I could see now that he was not much older than the 17-year-old Fournier twins who lived across the street from us.

"You play awfully good," I told him. "How come you are a hobo?"

"I didn't used to be,' he explained, "but we lost our ranch in Alberta and my dad took off to find work. I thought because I'm 18, that I should do the same. So here I am, trying to find work where there ain't none. I was hoping some grown-ups might come by and hear me play. Maybe they'd give me a couple of pennies or something. But I've been here all morning and haven't seen anyone but you two."

"Well we don't have any money," Clyde told him combatively, holding tightly onto the back of my shirt. "Neither does our dad."

Clyde was a year younger than I and much more aggressive. Even at six, he was quarrelsome. But usually only when he had mom or I to stand behind. The young hobo ignored his sassy attitude and grinned.

"I see you have a couple of fish, though," he said, looking at the two small fish dangling from the forked stick I was carrying. "How about we make a deal? We'll go into camp and cook those two whoppers on our big camp-fire. We can have a little feast and then I'll go back to the lake with you and help you catch some more that you can take home."

My mind raced. I liked him and he didn't seem much different than anybody else I knew. Besides, I had always wondered what the hobo jungle was like. But everybody said it was a very dangerous place.

"I'm afraid to go in there," I answered. "Mom told us not to talk with hobos."

"That's because she probably doesn't know any of us," he replied gently. "We don't do anybody any harm. All we want is somewhere we can be safe, cook the odd can of beans, and keep away from the railroad cops. Now, they are the guys you want to keep away from. They are really dangerous."

"But I've seen lots of those old hobos before and they're scary," I replied.

"Actually, most of them aren't old and scary at all," he told me For the most part they are all quite young. Some aren't much older than you and there are some that would be about your dad's age, but the majority are about like me."

Sensing my indecision, he added, "There isn't anyone who'll do you any harm. I guarantee it."

He looked at the fish.

"I've been thinking about how we are going to clean those fish. We don't have much water in there"

"We don't have to clean them," I said. "Dad often fries fish with the skin on. Sometimes he doesn't even take out the guts. When they are cooked the meat comes off the bones real easy."

"How about it, Clyde?" I asked. "It'd be fun to see the hobo jungle. We'd be the only kids in school that know what it's really like. Besides, the only reason we're going home right now is to eat the fish. Why not eat them here?"

Clyde just nodded and the hobo held out his hand.

"My name's Martin," he said. "Who are you guys?"

We told him our names and he put his mouth organ into

his mouth and played a few more head-bobbing, happy notes.

"Follow me," he said, and started up the trail, playing country singer Jimmy Rodger's hit song: *'Waiting for the Train'*.

"All Around the Water Tank
Waiting For a Train
A thousand Miles Away From Home
Sleeping in the Rain

I walked Up to a brakeman
To Give Him A Line of Talk
He says "If you've got Money
I'll see that you don't walk"

I haven't got a nickel
Not a penny can I show
He said Get off you Railroad Bum
And he slammed the box car door

My pocket book is empty
And my heart is filled with pain
I'm a thousand Miles away from home
Just waiting for a train"

The song was one of the biggest hits of the depression era, and has been recorded by many other great artists over the years, including Bazeny Cash, Hank Snow, and Jerry Lee Lewis.

I was surprised how short the trail was. The camp turned out to be within fifty feet or so of the street. It couldn't be seen because of the bushes and trees.

At first all I saw was an empty, well-trampled clearing with a big ring of large boulders in the center surrounded by a large number various sized logs. The trees and bushes around the clearing were decorated with all kinds of shirts, shorts, and socks. What I didn't see at first, were any of the hundreds of hobos that were said to live here, on and off, on their way to other cities.

As we walked toward the boulders though, I gradually began to pick out men sitting in the bushes, lounging in the shade of trees, brush piles, and small bits of canvas strung between small saplings and branches. Others lay on the ground using their back packs for pillows. Some waved when I looked at them, others ignored me completely. One guy got to his feet, picked up a guitar and headed over toward us.

"Hi there, Martin," he laughed. "I thought you were out there trying to raise money, not kids."

Martin had started to set fire to some dry sticks in the circle of big boulders that served as the community kitchen. There was a heavy iron grate on top of the rocks that he'd moved aside enough to get the fire going. An assortment of dented pots and pans sat on the edge of it. Others sat on the ground beside the fire pit boulders.

"Are you planning on cooking those boys, Martin?" the new comer asked. "They don't look fat enough to eat!"

Clyde's grip on the back of my shirt tightened. Suddenly, I was terrified. I looked at the two little perch. They weren't big enough for more than a couple of mouth fulls for the three of us.

"They really are going to eat us!" my mind screamed.

Martin's grin no longer seemed friendly. It looked more like he was licking his lips in anticipation of the banquet to come. Now I could see men moving in the bushes at the edge of the clearing. A few were already heading toward us, eyes fixed on me, wearing the same evil smiles that was pasted on Martin's handsome face. Only it didn't look handsome now. More like the Joker in the Batman comic books we liked to read in the grocery store.

They probably couldn't see Clyde now. He was pressed tightly against my back. I wanted to run, but I couldn't move. I think I tried, but Clyde was like a board on my back, holding me glued to the spot.

Then I heard Martin. "No," he was saying, "I caught myself a couple of fine perch, and invited these guys to help me eat them because they looked so hungry."

"Maybe they aren't going to eat us," I thought hopefully. "Maybe Martin is like Jesus. Maybe he can feed us and all these hungry hobos with those two fish."

I don't think Clyde was as worried about being cooked and eaten as was, because Martin's claim that he had caught the fish, triggered his naturally aggressive instincts.

"That's not true!" he yelled sticking his head out from behind my back to glare at Martin. "They are our fish."

"I'm sorry, Clyde," Martin apologized. "Old Baze and I are always spoofing one another, and sometimes we get stupid. They sure are your fish."

'Old Baze' was actually quite young. Probably the same age as Martin. But he was a lot bigger, with huge muscles that stretched the short sleeves of his tattered shirt. I thought again of Robin Hood and his 'merry men.' Here was Little Baze in person!

Clyde's head had quickly disappeared behind me again when Baze, whose real name was Basil, looked at him. Martin stepped closer and peered around me.

"Maybe if we got Baze to play and sing something, you wouldn't mind if he had a bite of fish too, would you Clyde?" Clyde nodded.

Now my fear had been replaced by confusion. I couldn't make decide which was the real Martin. Was he Jesus, who I was beginning to think was actually going to try feeding all the growing number of men moving in toward us with those two fish? Or was he the kind of hero who robbed the rich to feed the poor? I looked around for Friar Tuck.

Right now, the two fish only had to feed four people. Which was alright because there were two small fillets on each of them. But it was certainly beginning to look like there was going to be many more than four for lunch.

My musings were interrupted when 'Little Baze' began strumming and singing 'The Big Rock Candy Mountain'. I'd thought Martin was good, but Baze was great! So we sat on the logs that were scattered around the fire pit and listened to him while the fish cooked. Sometimes, if we knew some of the words, Clyde and I would join in. A dozen or so others had gathered around and sang along too. One of the men strummed an old banjo. A couple of men were taking advantage of the fire to cook beans and toasting bread on the iron grill, singing while they cooked. It began to look as if nobody was interested in eating Clyde and I. We were having too much fun.

When the fish were cooked, Martin cut out the filets with his knife and put them on a tin plate he'd retrieved from the pile on the ground near the rocks. He flung the remains to the squawking crows and gulls that had moved in to capitalize on the left-overs.

"Lunch is served," he announced, looking at Clyde and I. "Come and get it while it's hot!"

Baze joined us and we each took a piece of fish off the plate.

"That's all we get after all that hard work catching those fish?" Clyde asked.

"You think it's hard catching fish?" Baze asked. "Well you should try catching a freight car. Now that's HARD."

It was meant as a joke, but Martin seemed to take it seriously.

"That's for sure!" he said. "Lots of bos get badly hurt trying to hook onto trains. There have been lots of arms and legs left laying on the rails after a train has **passed**."

"What gets me," Baze interjected, "Is how some guys can stand riding the rods underneath the cars. I tried wrapping myself around them once and it was the scariest thing I've ever done. You're only inches from the railroad ties, going fifty miles an hour. And, if you think its comfortable just try laying on a couple of iron bars for four or five hours!"

By the time we got home, neither Clyde or I had any more fear of hobos. They were just ordinary men trying to survive under extra-ordinary circumstances. Canada was hit harder by the Great Depression than any other nation on earth. And the suffering peaked in northern Ontario.

What bothered my sleep now, was *becoming* a hobo and being trapped in an unheated boxcar in thirty below zero temperatures riding across the prairies. Brakemen have been known to deliberately lock the car doors knowing full well that the men trapped inside might freeze to death before anyone could let them out. For the same reason, ninety degree summer temperatures were equally deadly to men locked inside empty boxcars. Inside temperatures often soared to 130 or more suffocating degrees.

Then there the armed thugs who rode the boxcars pretending to be looking for work, when what they were really looking for was hobos to rob and terrorize. Many unsolved murders were committed in the dark corners of boxcars.

The railway police weren't much better. Many of them enjoyed breaking arms, legs, and heads with their nightsticks, for the sheer pleasure of it.

Chapter Twelve

The Hobo Jungle

Clyde and I had been fishing in the lake and were on our way home for lunch with a couple of perch that we'd caught when we met a hobo who, like the Pied Piper, played irresistable music, and we couldn't help ourselves from following him.

We'd just come up the trail to the end of Timmins Street when we saw him sitting on the ground a half-block away, near the path leading into the 'jungle'. He was playing hobo and train music on a mouth organ. They were songs we knew. Songs that dad always sang around the house; *'the wreck of the old number nine'*, *'the big rock candy mountain'*, *'Hallelujah, I'm a bum'*, and stuff like that. He was really good.

When we got too close we started edging over to the center of the road to make a wide arc around him. He quit playing and wiped his face with the red cowboy bandana he wore around his neck.

"Hello boys," he called. "Don't you like my music? It's hobo music because that's what I am now. I learned most of it riding the rails. Mostly from some of the other hobos. There's a lot of really good musicians *'riding the rods'*."

He smiled broadly and put the harmonica back in his mouth and played a few notes, twisting his head back and forth as he did, his stringy yellow hair flopping around his head. He looked at us and smiled.

We'd already guessed that he was a hobo from his ragged clothes and worn out shoes – just like ours – but he was different from all the old and scary bums we'd seen before. In spite of his short, straggly beard, I could see now that he was not much older than the 17-year-old Fournier twins who lived across the street from us.

"You play awfully good," I told him. "How come you are a hobo?"

"I didn't used to be,' he explained, "but we lost our ranch in Alberta and my dad took off to find work. I thought because I'm 17, that I should do the same. So here I am, trying to find work where there ain't none. I was hoping some grown-ups might come by and hear me play. Maybe they'd give me a couple of pennies or something. But I've been here all morning and haven't seen anyone but you two."

"Well we don't have any money," Clyde told him combatively, holding tightly onto the back of my shirt. "Neither does our dad."

Clyde was a year younger than I and much more aggressive. Even at six, he was quarrelsome..when he had mom or I to stand behind. The young hobo ignored his sassy attitude and grinned.

"I see you have a couple of fish, though," he said, looking at the two small fish dangling from the forked stick I was carrying. "How about we make a deal? We'll go into camp and cook those two whoppers on our big camp-fire. We can have a little feast and then I'll go back to the lake with you and help you catch some more that you can take home."

My mind raced. I liked him and he didn't seem much different than anybody else I knew. Besides, I had always wondered what the hobo jungle was like. But everybody said it was a very dangerous place.

"I'm afraid to go in there," I answered. "Mom told us not

to talk with hobos."

"That's because she probably doesn't know any of us," he replied gently. "We don't do anybody any harm. All we want is somewhere we can be safe, cook the odd can of beans, and keep away from the railroad cops. Now, there are some guys you want to keep away from. They are really dangerous."

"But I've seen lots of those old hobos before and they're scary."

"Actually, most of them aren't old and scary at all. For the most part they are all quite young. Some aren't much older than you and some would be about your dad's age, but the majority are about like me."

Sensing my indecision, he added, "There isn't anyone who'll do you any harm. I guarantee it."

He looked at the fish.

"I've been thinking about how we are going to clean those fish. We don't have much water in there"

"We don't have to clean them," I said. "Dad often fries fish with the skin on. Sometimes he doesn't even take out the guts. When they are cooked the meat comes off the bones real easy."

"How about it, Clyde?" I asked. "It'd be fun to see the hobo jungle. We'd be the only kids in school to know what it's really like. Besides, the only reason we're going home right now is to eat the fish. Why not eat them here?"

Clyde just nodded and the hobo held out his hand.

"My name's Martin," he said. "Who are you guys?"

We told him our names and he put his mouth organ into his mouth and played a few more head-bobbing, happy notes.

"Follow me," he said, and started up the trail, playing country singer Jimmy Rodger's hit song: *'Waiting for the Train'*.

> "All Around the Water Tank
> Waiting For a Train
> A thousand Miles Away From Home
> Sleeping in the Rain
>
> I walked Up to a brakeman
> To Give Him A Line of Talk
> He says "If you've got Money
> I'll see that you don't walk"
>
> I haven't got a nickel
> Not a penny can I show
> He said Get off you Railroad Bum
> And he slammed the box car door
>
> My pocket book is empty
> And my heart is filled with pain
> I'm a thousand Miles away from home
> Just waiting for a train"

The song was one of the biggest hits of the depression era, and has been recorded by many other great artists over the years, including Bazeny Cash, Hank Snow, and Jerry Lee Lewis.

I was surprised how short the trail was. The camp turned out to be within fifty feet or so of the street. It just couldn't be seen because of the bushes and trees.

At first all I saw was an empty, well-trampled clearing with a big ring of large boulders in the center surrounded by a large number various sized logs. The trees and bushes around the clearing were decorated with all kinds of shirts, shorts, and socks. What I didn't see at first, were any of the hundreds of hobos that were said to live here, on and off, on their way to other cities.

As we walked toward the boulders though, I gradually began to pick out men sitting in the bushes, lounging in the shade of trees, brush piles, and small bits of canvas strung between small saplings and branches. Other men lay on the ground using their back packs for pillows. Some waved when I looked at them, others ignored me completely. One guy got to his feet, picked up a guitar and headed over toward us.

"Hi there, Martin," he laughed. "I thought you were out there trying to raise money, not kids."

Martin had started to set fire to some dry sticks in the circle of big boulders that served as the community kitchen. There was a heavy iron grate on top of the rocks that he'd moved aside enough to get the fire going. An assortment of dented pots and pans sat on the edge of it. Others sat on the ground beside the fire pit boulders.

"Are you planning on cooking those boys, Martin?" the new comer asked. "They don't look fat enough to eat!"

Clyde's grip on the back of my shirt tightened. Suddenly, I was terrified. I looked the two little perch. They weren't big enough for more than a couple of mouth fulls for the three of us.

"They really are going to eat us!" my mind screamed.

Martin's grin no longer seemed friendly. It looked more like he was licking his lips in anticipation of the banquet to come. Now I could see men moving in the bushes at the edge of the clearing. A few were already heading toward us, eyes fixed on me, wearing the same evil smiles that was pasted on Martin's handsome face. Only it don't look handsome now. More like the Joker in the Batman comic books we liked to read in the grocery store.

They probably couldn't see Clyde now. He was pressed tightly against my back. I wanted to run, but I couldn't move. I think I tried, but Clyde was like a board on my back, holding me glued to the spot.

Then I heard Martin. "No," he was saying, "I caught myself a couple of fine perch, and invited these guys to help me eat them because they looked so hungry."

"Maybe they aren't going to eat us," I thought hopefully. "Maybe Martin is like Jesus. Maybe he can feed us and all these hungry hobos with those two fish."

I don't think Clyde was as worried about being cooked and eaten as was, because Martin's claim that he had caught the fish, triggered Clyde's naturally combative instincts.

"That's not true!" he yelled sticking his head out from behind my back to glare at Martin. "They are our fish."

"I'm sorry, Clyde," Martin apologized. "Old Baze and I are always spoofing one another, and sometimes we get stupid. They sure are your fish."

'Old Baze' was actually quite young. Probably the same age as Martin. But he was a lot bigger, with huge muscles that stretched the short sleeves of his tattered shirt. I thought again Robin Hood and his 'merry men.' Here was Little Baze in person!

Clyde's head had quickly disappeared behind me again when Baze, whose real name was Basil, looked at him. Martin stepped closer and peered around me.

"Maybe if we got Baze to play and sing something, you wouldn't mind if he had a bite of fish too, would you Clyde." Clyde nodded.

Now my fright had been replaced by confusion. I couldn't make decide which was the real Martin. Was he Jesus, who I was beginning to think was actually going to try feeding all the growing number of men moving in toward us with those two fish? Or was he the hero Robin Hood, who robbed the rich to feed the poor? I looked around for Friar Tuck.

Right now, the two fish only had to feed four people.

Which was alright because there were two small filets on each of them. But it was certainly beginning to look like there was going to be many more than four for lunch.

My musings were interrupted when Baze began strumming and singing 'The Big Rock Candy Mountain'. I'd thought Martin was good, but Baze was great! So we sat on the logs that were scattered around the fire pit and listened to him while the fish cooked. Sometimes, if we knew some of the words, Clyde and I would join in. A dozen or so others had gathered around and sang along. One of the men strummed an old banjo. A couple of men were taking advantage of the fire to cook beans and toasting bread on the iron grill, singing while they cooked. It began to look as if nobody was interested in eating Clyde and I. We were having too much fun.

When the fish were cooked, Martin cut out the fillets with his knife and put them on a tin plate he retrieved from the pile on the ground near the rocks. He flung the remains to the squawking crows and gulls that had moved in to capitalize on the leftovers.

"Lunch is served," he announced, looking at Clyde and I. "Come and get it while it's hot!"

Baze joined us and we each took a piece of fish off the plate.

"That's all we get after all that hard work catching those fish?" Clyde asked.

"You think it's hard catching fish?" Baze asked. "Well you should try catching a freight car. Now that's HARD."

It was meant as a joke, but Martin seemed to take it seriously.

"That's for sure!" he said. "Lots of bos get badly hurt trying to hook onto trains. There have been lots of arms and legs left laying on the rails after a train has passed."

"What gets me," Baze interjected, "Is how some guys can stand riding the rods underneath the cars. I tried wrapping myself around them once and it was the scariest thing I've ever done. You're only inches from the railroad ties going fifty miles an hour. And, if you think its comfortable just try laying on a couple of iron bars for four or five hours!"

By the time we got home, neither Clyde or I had any more fear of hobos. They were just ordinary men trying to survive under extra-ordinary circumstances. Canada was hit harder by the Great Depression than any other nation on earth. And the suffering peaked in northern Ontario.

What bothered my sleep now, was *becoming* a hobo and being trapped in an unheated boxcar in thirty below zero temperatures riding across the prairies. Brakemen have been known to deliberately lock the car doors knowing full well that the men trapped inside might freeze to death before anyone could let them out. For the same reason, ninety degree summer temperatures were equally deadly to men locked inside empty boxcars. Inside temperatures often soared to 130 or more suffocating degrees.

Then there the armed thugs who rode the boxcars pretending to be looking for work, when what they were really looking for was hobos to rob and terrorize. Many unsolved murders were committed in the dark corners of boxcars.

The railway police weren't much better. Many of them enjoyed breaking arms, legs, and heads with their nightsticks, for the sheer pleasure of it.

Chapter Thirteen
BULL FIGHT

We encountered a couple of 'Bulls' in the swimming hole under the CNR railway bridge that crossed Duchesnay Creek about two miles west of our house on Timmins Street. We often walked there often to catch red-fin suckers, or to play in Duchesnay Falls, or to swim in the deep, slow-moving water under the railway bridge.

We'd walk the rails, search for spikes lost by the 'Gandy Dancers' when they were building the railroad during World War One, and pick the wild strawberries the grew along the embankment. Sometimes we'd shoot stones at the glass insulators on the telegraph poles with our slingshots.

> **Note:** Gandy Dancer is a term applied to railway construction workers of long ago. It comes from the long-handled shovel they used in their work. Made by the Gandy Manufacturing Company in Chicago, it was strong enough to use as a pry bar. The shovel blade could be inserted under a heavy iron rail and the worker would bounce on the handle's end to shift the rail into place. Thus the term 'Gandy Dancer'.

The chances of us hitting an insulator with a slingshot were actually very slim, but every once in a while, someone would score, and put a little chip in the heavy glass. We didn't think we were doing any harm, but I guess it must have caused some sort of disruption in telegraph communications because it that was the reason for the confrontation between Rene and the Railway Police.

We were splashing and yelling in the pool under the bridge, when two guys in suits walked down the path from the tracks and yelled at us.

"What are you kids doing here?" one of the men asked. "This is railway property and you are trespassing."

"What does it look like we're doing?" Rene Fournier asked loudly. He was only nine, but he wasn't afraid of anybody, mostly because his two older brothers always backed him up. They played on defense with the North Bay's Junior A hockey team and loved to fight. They were also their team's most penalized players.

"Besides, this creek doesn't belong to the railway" Rene added. "So just leave us alone!"

No one ever talked to the railroad police like that. They busted open hobo heads with their billy clubs for a lot less than that. One of them flipped back his lapel and pointed to his shield.

"If you don't get out of there right now, I'll throw the whole lot of you in jail," he roared.

I was scared, but Rene wasn't about to back down.

"You and what army?" he screamed. "You got no right to bully kids that aren't doing nothing. Why don't you just go and chase some hobos? That's all you guys are good for."

That was too much. The two men jumped into the water, clothes and all. But we had already backed away to safety on the other side of the creek. Now as the two men waded through the deep water toward us, we raced to shore and ran down toward the highway, leaving them floundering and cursing in the water.

The last I saw, a group of adults who had been attracted by the shouting, were standing talking with two dripping men, who finally climbed out of the water trudged back back up the hill to the tracks.

We waited near the highway awhile, then went cautiously-back to where we'd ditched our clothes earlier and walked safely home by way of Main Street. No railway tracks for us this time.

A couple of days later, Constable Green distributed a letter to people in the neighborhood, asking them to warn their children that breaking glass insulators endangered everyone in the community by disrupting electricity and telephone service.

Chapter Fourteen
THE LONG ARM OF THE LAW

Let's be clear about it right up front. I knew it was wrong to steal vegetables from someone's garden. And I had often seen the no-trespassing signs posted on the fence. I also knew that if we got caught we'd be in big trouble. But I was hungry and my stomach had preempted my brain. All I could think of was those big red tomatoes hanging from the vines.

It never even crossed my mind that some of the hungry men in the hobo jungle a couple of blocks away might have already visited this particular garden. If it had, I probably would have deduced that the garden was well protected by some sort of effective security system: anything from a couple of German Shepherds to trip-wired shotguns.

Clyde, being only seven, didn't think of it either. There were no street lights in the area and the garden was dark. The fence was low and easy to climb over. The tomatoes were fairly close, and the gardener's house was dark. The night was quiet.

"Don't take too much, Clyde," I whispered. "We gotta be fast. Just feel your way around and pick a few of whatever you can find and get the heck out of there."

"OK," he answered in a tight voice. "Let's go before somebody comes."

The fence wire squeaked as we climbed over it into the garden, but everything else remained quiet.

"That was easy," I thought, as I crouched and moved toward the black shapes of the tomato plants ahead. But disaster came too quickly; like a bolt of lightning. Floodlights blazed on, turning the garden into a brightly lit Colosseum with two terrified Christians about to be fed to the lions.

Clyde's leg had hit a trip wire before either of us had a chance to pick a single tomato. We stood paralyzed with fear as a big man came running toward us with a rifle.

"Don't move a muscle, boys," he yelled. "I don't want to shoot you."

The man lowered the barrel of the rifle and clicked the safety on when he saw we were only children.

"What in blazes are you boys doing out at this time of night?" he asked. "You should have been in bed a long time ago."

Clyde was crying and didn't answer.

I told him that we were in bed, but we were hungry thought we'd sneak out and get some tomatoes. We passed here often and knew your tomatoes were ripe.

"You've got so many that I didn't think you'd miss a few. We only wanted enough to share with our little sisters," I explained.

"Where do you live?" the man asked.

I was so worried about what was going to happen to us that I had to ask him what he meant.

"You must live in house," he said. You told me you were in bed. Where is your bed?"

I was trying to keep from crying. "It's in our room, next to mom and dad's," I answered.

Just then saw the flashing red lights of a police car

coming toward us a few blocks away and my fear exploded into tears. "Are you going to send us to jail?" I sobbed.

"I don't know," he answered, "That's up to the police. Does your mom and dad know you are here?" he wanted to know.

"No. We snuck out" I answered.

The police car came to a stop in front of the house and the man walked us over to meet the policeman.

"You boys get into the back seat here," he said, and opened the door for us. "I want to talk with Mr. Pendrell, then we'll take a ride downtown and get to the bottom of this."

As we climbed in, he told us gruffly that he wouldn't put handcuffs on us "if you promise you won't try to escape."

We got to the police station a half hour later and were taken to an empty cell and thoroughly interrogated and intimidated by our captor, Officer Greene, and a couple of other policemen.

They'd question us for a few minutes, then one of them would go into another room, leaving the others silently standing guard, glaring at us with hands on their holstered weapons. Then the first officer would come back, whisper to the others, then go through the questioning routine again. Finally, After threatening long jail terms and foster homes, they agreed to let us go if we promised never, ever, to steal anything again.

We quickly and enthusiastically promised and Officer Greene drove us back to Mr. Pendrell's house.

"What are we doing here?" I whispered to Clyde. Then, as we came to a stop, Mr. Pendrell came out carrying a big potato sack . He opened the back door of the car, and put the sack on the seat beside me.

"Give this to your parents," he told me, "and tell them I said not to be too hard on you. I expect you've had enough for one night."

Officer Greene pounded on our door to wake mom and dad who were almost as shocked as we had been earlier when the garden lights flashed on. After a short private talk with Officer Greene, and seeing the generous gift of vegetables from Mr. Pendrell, they said we'd talk in the morning. They gave us each a tomato from the sack and sent us to bed. It was long past our bedtime.

I had a close call with the law again the following month, a few days after school started in September. An older kid named Ernie Warren showed up at my house on Saturday morning with a new bike his uncle had given him to ride to and from school.

"Can you ride a bike?" he asked me. "My uncle gave me this, but I don't know how to ride it."

I told him I had never ridden one either, but I'd hold the bike to help him keep his balance while he tried to learn.

After a half hour of failed attempts, he told me he didn't think he'd ever be able to ride and said he thought he'd take it down to a second-hand store on Oak street and sell it. Money would be better than a bicycle he couldn't ride.

It sounded like a good idea to me. Especially when he said he'd give me a dollar from the sale if I went with him. I agreed and told mom I was going down town with Ernie and we'd be back in an hour.

The owner of the very first store we went into said he was interested and would give Ernie $10 for it.

"It's a good looking bike sonny," he said, "Do you have a sales permit?"

"What's that?" Ernie asked. "How much does it cost? Where can I get one?"

"It's nothing really," the man replied. "It doesn't cost anything. You just go to the police station and give them your name and address. They'll record it and get you to sign saying that you own the bike. Then you'll get a copy to show to me."

On the way to the police station, Ernie said, "We can't take the bike into the police station so you go in and get the sales permit. I'll stay outside and make sure nobody steals it. I'll give you an extra dollar for doing it."

I was very nervous going into the office after my previous experience and wondered if I should give them my real address. After all, I wasn't actually a salesman, and didn't own the bike.

"Hello son," an officer said. "What can I do for you?"

"I need to get a sales permit," I answered.

He got out a piece of paper and said, "Ok. What's your name and address?"

This is going to be easy I thought.

"Calvin Smith. Toronto," I said. He wrote that down.

"What street in Toronto?" he asked.

I didn't know any streets in Toronto but being a very fast thinker, I said "Main Street."

"What number on Main Street?"

"I forgot," I replied. He wrote something down.

"OK," he said. "Now, what is it that you sell?"

"Bicycles," I answered.

Just then Officer Greene appeared in the door from

another room.

"Well hello Calvin," he greeted me.

Suddenly my mouth got very dry and a whole jumble of thoughts started screaming in my head. I couldn't think or hear anything. I guess I stammered some kind of hello.

The next thing I knew, I was in his office and he was kneeling on the floor beside me.

"Calm down Calvin. don't be frightened." he said. "I know you haven't done anything wrong. But somebody has and I just have to know what's going on."

I told him the whole story and he asked me where Ernie was now. Just then the outer door opened and Ernie walked into the office. I heard him ask the desk officer if a boy had come in to get a sales permit.

The officer said, "Yes come right this way."

Ernie's goose was cooked. Apparently he had stolen the bike and everybody had known it but me. Officer Greene drove me home for the second time that summer. Ernie stayed at the station. I have no idea what happened after I left, but I never saw him again. He had never been a close friend and he never went back to King George Elementary school.

When Halloween came that year, dad felt really bad because he couldn't afford to buy us any fireworks. So he did the next best thing, which was to make some himself. When we returned from 'trick or treating' he announced his plan.

"I'll get a couple of my .32 rifle bullets and we'll open them and take out the gunpowder." he said. "Then we'll burn it In the yard. It should make a pretty good flash. It will only be one, but that's better than none, eh?"

We all thought it was a good idea. We'd never seen

gunpowder before and it sounded dangerous, and therefor Ideal for Halloween.

"But there's something else we can do too," he continued. "I found a piece of iron in my toolbox that you kids can file down to make some sparklers. I'll show you how."

He put a file and an old metal hinge on a paper he had spread on the table and told Clyde and I to take turns filing it.

"Make sure all the filings stay on the paper," he warned. "We're going to need all you can get."

Even the two girls took turns with the file. It was really difficult without a vice to hold the piece of metal, and they didn't produce a lot but they had fun trying. Clyde surprised everybody except mom, by actually doing his share of the work.

While we were making metal filings, dad sat at the opposite side of the table where we could watch him remove the lead from the two bullets with his jack knife and pour the powder onto a piece of paper. Then he mixed some of the metal bits in with it. Afterward, we sliced pieces of cedar kindling wood into thin sticks, gave them a light coating of glue, and sprinkled them with the rest of the filings.

Outside, our final products – the result of an hour and a half of hard work and great fun – hissed and sparked for a few seconds then went out. Halloween had been an awesome success!

When winter arrived, Art and Eugene Fournier, Rene's 18-year-old hockey playing twin brothers gave us their old sticks to play with on the snow-covered street. We had no hockey pucks but that was no problem. There was an unlimited supply of frozen horse manure (called, logically enough, 'horse puckies') on the streets.

Dogs were allowed to run free in those days and

competed with us, and each other, for the make-do pucks. Unlike us, they didn't fight or try to score goals, but they didn't play fair either. Whenever they got the puck, they ate it. We'd have to call time-out to look for a replacement.

Most families made skating rinks in their back yards in the cold weather. It was simply a matter of clearing a reasonable-sized patch of snow and piling it up along four sides to create an embankment and then flooding it with a garden hose. It sometimes took days to run enough water to make a patch large and smooth enough to skate on. As you could guess, the day it was ready, it would snow again, and the patch would have to be shoveled off.

Cecile Levesque lived next door to us for a while. She loved to yodel while she skated. She was highly talented at both. In my opinion she made Hank the Yodeling Ranger sound like a Leghorn rooster.

She was my age and being an only child, her parents not only made an exceptionally large rink for her, but rigged up flood lights so she could skate at night. I can't remember why, but she had very few friends. The neighbor girls didn't seem to like her and no boy would be caught dead playing with a girl. So Cecile skated alone, yodeling mournfully in the moon and flood lights.

Then one day it snowed very hard and all of the neighborhood rinks were buried too deep for recovery. Cecile couldn't skate any more.

But Timmins Street runs uphill all the way from its beginning near the lake to Jane Street above us, and the heavy snow made the street ideal for sliding on toboggans and flattened cardboard boxes. It also made it impossible for cars to climb the hill and very difficult for horses; which made it safe for us. Before long, even while the storm still raged, the street was packed with kids sliding down the hill on toboggans, sleighs, skis, and flattened cardboard boxes.

A lady my mother cleaned house for had given us a small toboggan that her grown-up children didn't use any more. Jeri, Clyde, and I were taking turns sliding down the hill with it when Cecile came out to the road in her snowsuit and stood quietly watching.

Jeri had just started up the hill dragging the toboggan and Clyde and I were heaving snowballs at each other. When I noticed her watching, I grinned, yelled "Hi", and tossed a snowball her way. When she threw one back at me and almost hit Clyde, it triggered a free-for-all that ended with her taking turns with us on the toboggan and cardboard boxes.

The four of us played together until we got too wet and cold to stay out any longer. By that time however, Cecile had become queen of the hill, yodeling her way to popularity with all the kids in the neighborhood.

The snow continued on and off all winter. The snow plows pushed it up into six to eight-foot banks, along both sides of the streets. This provided us with a wonderful new resource for fun. We had long since tired of building snowmen and forts, so now we dug into the snowbanks and made caves and tunnels that ran for half a block.

Neighborhood parents could no longer look out of their windows and see their kids playing on the streets. So they too, had to bundle up and crawl through snow tunnels in order to find them. Soon, some of the tunnels were even furnished with small chairs and tables. Toys were scattered throughout. We got a very realistic taste of Eskimo life.

My mother crawled in one day looking for Clyde and found Mrs. Doyle coming from the other direction. They spent the rest of the morning gossiping happily in the warm soft light of the cavern.

Outside of the tunnels, temperatures had dropped

sharply to an average of -11F degrees and Lake Nippissing had frozen over. The all-time low of -40F for December/January established in the late 1800s, was often closely tested that winter.

Ice-fishing huts dotted the frozen surface of Lake Nippissing and would remain there until late April when the warm air made the ice too soft for safety. Long before then though, the North Bay Ice and Coal Company's storage sheds would be packed to the ceiling with sawdust covered, six-foot square blocks that had been cut from the lake and hauled into storage by horses. During the summer the huge slabs would be carved into twelve equal squares which would be sold for 25 cents each for use in ice-boxes through the city. The delivery men were paid 10 cents an hour and worked 10 hours a day, 6 days a week.

Although electric refrigerators had been available in North Bay long before 1938, not many people owned them. They were too expensive. As many as 45 percent of Canadians were unemployed and monthly relief payments varied from $19 in Halifax to $60 in Calgary. Many of those who were employed, were paid as little as fifty cents a day. Even in 1942, when I got my first job at the age of 12, my wages were only $2 for ten hours of hard labor.

With such a poor economy, there weren't an awful lot of people who could take advantage of Eaton's low $278 cash sale price on the new Fridgidaire Coldwall models in 1936. You could almost buy a new car for that much. The sale was a flop even after they offered terms with just $5 down. Thus, North Bay Ice and Coal would remain in business until the economy picked up after World War II.

We kids were quite happy without refrigerators. We liked the slow-moving horse-drawn ice-wagons coming down the street on the hot summer days with free ice chunks for everyone. They were the closest thing to ice cream that we ever saw and the drivers knew it. They always made sure they had plenty of ice-chips ready for our eager hands. Sometimes, when the customer's ice-box couldn't handle a whole block, and the driver had to cut one to size with his ice-pick, he'd make sure there were lots of big chips to give to the special children he liked. But Rene Fournier wasn't one of them.

Chapter Fifteen
GUNS AND WHISTLES

North Bay may be plagued with trillions of shadflies for three weeks every year but the benefits derived from them are incalculable. They are the base for one of the best fresh water sport fisheries in Canada, bringing in millions of tourist dollars every year.

Contrarily, the Timmins Street ghetto was plagued with even greater numbers of the world's most annoying and harmful flying insects: the whining, blood-sucking mosquitoes that poison countless people and animals all over the world every year. Most sections of North Bay were mosquito-free, but here, on the edge of town, we suffered with them from April to September.

Unlike shadfles, which have no mouths or stingers, mosquitoes do nothing but suck blood from people and animals every night from dusk to dawn, Then, when the sun comes up in the morning,, they go into hiding to make way for the clouds of another predatory parasite: the blackfly. It chews out chunks of flesh to create blood 'spings' that it drinks freely from, then poisons to infect its host.

If it came to a contest for evil between the two little monsters, blackflies would probably win for torture infliction, while the mosquito would take home the prize for disease transmission. But the race would be very close in both categories. Mosquitoes inject poisons and infectious microbes into your system with the same hollow needle they use to suck out your blood. Blackflies inflict a painful gash to create a blood pool, then stand on the edge of it lapping up the blood like jackals at a jungle watering hole.

Fortunately, black flies require fast-flowing water for their eggs, and the nearest creek to us on Timmins Street was Duchesnay Creek, two miles away. So, although they inflicted more damage than their vampiric cousins, not as many of them ventured as far from their birth place as Timmins Street.

On the other hand, our neighborhood provided an ideal habitat for the mosquitoes. They liked to lay their eggs in the tall grasses, weeds, rainwater-filled bottles, cans, tires, etc. that were scattered here in great abundance. We even had a large stagnant pond at the end of the street, that boiled off clouds of freshly hatched mosquitoes every evening.

Mosquitoes weren't the only flying insects that filled the night-time skies though. The dull lights of our houses attracted an infinite number of fireflies, June bugs, and moths – which allowed me to accumulate the biggest and best moth collection in my class at school. The June bugs and moths attracted a lot of bats, which, although harmless to people, frightened some of the neighborhood girls. Their mothers thought the little sonar-guided animals might get tangled in their hair.

I like bats and did my best to keep the other kids from trying to catch them with their butterfly nets. But there was nothing I could do though to keep them from crashing into screen doors that their sonar couldn't detect. Or to prevent nighthawks and owls from swooping in to kill and carry them away for a midnight feast.

God has an infinite number of ways to bring his children to a grisly end. What's even worse is that he often uses kids to do his nasty work for him. Even I often went down to the pond at the end of the street to gather frogs eggs and catch polywogs in glass jars. We didn't eat frog's eggs or polywogs, and they don't make great pets in glass pickle jars, so whatever we took from the pond ended up rotting on the ground somewhere. Don't ask me why I took them from the pond. If I was religious, I would say that the Devil made me do it, or God, whichever one had the most power. I certainly wouldn't have done it on my own.

It was a very dangerous pass-time. Particularly in bare feet. We often got glass cuts, most of which became infected. One time I stepped on a jar bottom with long jagged shards that sliced deep into the ball of my foot and required a dozen stitches. Fortunately doctors still hadn't abandoned the practice of making house calls, and one of them got to our house before I lost too much blood.

The frogs we tried to kill were actually in less danger than we were. Although we tried hard to pick them off with our slingshots, we rarely ever hit one. Not that we weren't good shots. They were just too hard to spot in the weeds and cat-tails, and moved faster than the rocks we shot at them. As soon as they heard the snap of the rubber bands, they ducked under the water and disappeared.

Our slingshots were all home-made, constructed from Y-shaped tree branches, strips of discarded inner tubes, and leather pads cut from the tongues of the old shoes we found in the garbage piles behind the houses. We spent a lot of time searching those treasure piles for things we could use to make stuff like rubber-band guns, bows and arrows, and hide-outs with.

Although our feet got heavily calloused from going barefoot most of the time during the summer months, we never strayed off the streets, railway tracks, or the well-worn paths. Even so, we suffered the odd stubbed toe, wood sliver, and small glass cut, but more serious foot injuries were uncommon.

It was a different story when we wanted to go into the fields and garbage piles. Agony and death threatened our every step. Venturing there without shoes was akin to wading in the snake and 'gator filled swamps of Georgia. Nobody would dare hunt for treasure there without shoes, even if it was only a worn-out second-hand pair. There were shards of broken glass and jagged edged tin cans laying everywhere in the no-man's land behind the houses. All of them just waiting to inflict mortal wounds on the unwary.

Just as scratch is all it takes in the unsanitary conditions that existed in our area. The place had no equal for its rich bacteria cultures. Even a minor bloodless puncture wound often resulted in lockjaw from the tetanus bacteria. Gangrene doesn't only affect amputees, any cut can become gangrenous. Necrotizing subcutaneous infections, which result from another lethal bacteria, can develop into gangrene, and the Clostridium bacteria produces 'gas gangrene'.

With care, however, the place was also a poor kids Aladdin's treasure grotto. There may not have been much gold in the garbage piles, but they were filled with everything we needed to make anything our imaginations can contrive. It's where we got rubber and leather for our slingshots, scrap wood to carve our guns, feathers for our Indian headdresses, tin cans for worms, glass jars for polywogs, string for fishing lines, wild cucumbers for hand grenades, sweaters for knitting yarn, and much, much more. The place was a magnet that we couldn't resist.

Wild cucumber vines grew like ivy over garbage heaps, shrubs, fences and outhouses. The fruit was inedible but their soft skin made made them perfect exploding hand grenades. The spines look sharp, but are very soft and harmless.

Wild cucumbers look prickly but the spines are soft

We played cowboys and Indians by running around with tin cans stuck to our worn-out shoes to imitate the clacking of horse hooves, and shot each other with rubber bands propelled from gun-shaped pieces of wood. We made the trigger mechanisms from spring clothespins attached to the handles.

One end of the rubber band 'bullet' was inserted into the jaws of the clothespin and stretched over the end of the 'barrel'. When the 'trigger' was pressed the rubber band flew off the gun toward the target. Extra distance could be achieved by either wrapping the jaws of the clothespin with inner tube rubber, or lengthening the barrel to increase tension on the bullet.

My dad showed me how to make make a great whistle one spring day while we were fishing trout in the North River near Widdifield Station.

He wanted to move a little way upstream, but I was getting lots of nibbles where I was and didn't want to leave. "Well you stay here," he told me, "and just whistle if you need me. I won't be very far."

"I can't whistle very loud, dad," I reminded him.

"Yeah," he admitted. "I'll just make you a police whistle. It'll only take a couple of minutes"

Taking out his pocket knife, he walked over to a small poplar tree and cut off a half-inch diameter branch and sat down on a rock beside me.

"You can't make these in the summer-time. Only in spring when the sap is running, and only with aspen, poplar, and birch branches," he told me. "The sap goes up the branches between the bark and the wood making it easy to slide the bark off in one piece."

In just a couple of minutes he'd made me a whistle that I valued much more than anything we could have bought at any sport shop. Soon every kid in the neighborhood had a poplar whistle and all of our parents were being whistled slowly crazy.

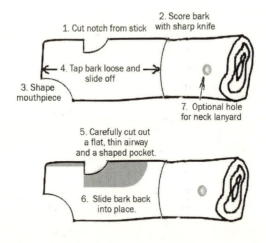

We made many of our own playthings – with some ideas and a little assistance from our parents, of course. We salvaged the metal rings that held wooden barrels together (barrel hoops) and rolled them up and down the street with 'hoop sticks' made from two sticks nailed together in the shape of an upside-down cross.

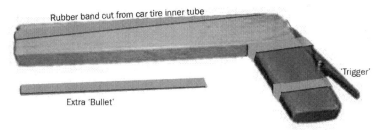

A finished rubber band gun. Guns were usually one piece of wood shaped with a coping saw. Otherwise parental help was required to dowel and glue a separate handle onto the barrel.

It was a lot of fun making things, and we were always proud of our handiwork.

Chapter Sixteen
PADDY'S LAKESIDE CASINO

Uneducated and unskilled, my father worked at hard-labor jobs the first four years after he quit school. In so doing, he developed a hard, muscular physique that by the time he turned eighteen, qualified him to work as a waiter/bouncer in the beer parlors of the local hotels. He was tough when he needed to be, but he also had a very pleasant personality and made friends easily. One of them was a guard at the North Bay jail named Joe Ranger.

Joe wasn't as tall as dad, but he was strong and very quick with his fists. Dad, in his duties as a bouncer, constantly battling with drunken toughs, soon earned the reputation of being a dangerous guy to mess with. With their similar good looks and brawling abilities they fit well together. Both very handsome, pleasant to be around, and perfectly able to protect themselves and their friends when challenged – which was seldom. They soon became almost inseparable, drinking, chasing girls, and playing pool and poker together.

One of their favorite poker games was run by one of dad's best friends; a one-legged, one-eyed, ex-miner named Paddy Inman. Paddy had lost an eye and leg in a coal-mine explosion in Glace Bay, Nova Scotia in 1903. After he recovered from his injuries, he got a job cleaning the local pool room. When business was slow, he and his boss would play for pennies and pretty soon, in spite of having just one eye, Paddy became a pool 'shark' and his reputation grew. With his eye-patch and crutches, he could out-hustle the hustlers who found it difficult to believe that a one-eyed cripple could be as good as he seemed to think he was. And so his bank-roll grew.

He soon began to travel to other Nova Scotia towns and cities where people didn't know him and started making serious money. Then, one evening in a pool room in North Bay, the guy he was playing with became furious over losing a large wager and struck Paddy across the side of the head with his pool cue. He was taken to the hospital with a concussion, a fractured cheek bone, and blurred the vision in his good eye. The stranger who hit him simply walked out of the pool hall without paying the table fees, or his debt to Paddy, and disappeared.

Paddy's pool playing days were over. When he got out of the hospital, he moved into a downtown hotel, bought himself a bamboo pole and a fishing line and started hanging out on the government dock, fishing for wall eyes (pickerel). When his money began to dwindle, he got some scrap lumber and built a shack on the beach near the dock and moved out of the hotel.

He loved fishing and his new passion soon developed into a lucrative business, renting bamboo fishing poles and selling live minnows and worms to the hundreds of anglers who crowded the wharf every day to catch the pickerel, pike, and perch that lived and thrived in this miracle lake.

Paddy kept his prices low, so his business got better and better. Most of his customers were too poor to buy tubular metal rods, expensive level-wind reels, and colorful artificial lures. All they cared about was catching enough fish to feed their families at the lowest possible cost, and Paddy's bamboo poles worked just fine for doing that.

In the early morning when the fish were hungriest, and eagerly gobbled the injured minnows hooked on the end of the cotton fishing lines dangling from bamboo poles off the dock, Paddy had a hard time keeping up with the demand for bait (minnows and dew worms) and frequently hired the boys who hung around the dock to wade the shallow water near shore and net the silver-scaled shiners that schooled there. He loaned them fine-mesh seine nets and paid them two cents a dozen for all they could catch. By 7:00 the water in his home-made wooden bait tank would be crowded with flashing silver minnows, the boys' pockets would be jingling with pennies, and every minnow pail on the dock would be well stocked with the little bait fish.

He made a lot of money, and a lot of new friends, with his little fisherman supply business. Some of his customers, my dad included, often came back in the evening to play checkers and cards with him. Before long, many of his friends had expressed enough interest in playing poker for pennies that he organized a Saturday night game, and the little shack gradually became a poor man's 'casino on the beach', open seven nights a week.

At dusk, Paddy would chain his bamboo poles to the side of the building, lock the cover of the minnow box, and fire up the coal-oil lamps in his tiny home-come-poker palace. Soon afterward, his guests would arrive with their pennies, nickels, dimes, and the occasional dollar bill. He was often forced to turn people away because of the limited seating capacity of his small shack. It could hold only one table and eight chairs.

Paddy not only played in the games, but he was also the dealer, making it impossible for him to lose. As in all casinos, the 'house' is entitled to a small rake-off from every pot. Paddy was the house and wasn't greedy, so nobody complained.

One of the regulars was a disbarred lawyer named Michael McRae, who happened to know that the town hall in Fort Worth, Texas, had burned down in 1905, which was the year of my father's birth. He said all dad would have to do to claim US citizenship was to say he was born in Fort Worth in '05 but had never been issued with a birth certificate.

Whether or not it was true, the story was good enough to

give him unhindered access to the States and a job in a shingle factory on the U.S. side of Niagara Falls. It was also good enough for the Tonnawanda birth records office. Fort Worth is officially recorded on my birth certificate as the city of my father's birth.

I often went with my dad to Paddy's poker games. Being only seven I didn't play of course, but it was fun watching and listening to the players' chit-chat in the dim light of the two coal-oil lamps mounted on the walls near the table. With all the hours I spent watching, I couldn't help but learn the rules of the game, the relative rank of the hands, how to play tight, when to bluff, and when to fold.

After a month or so of going to Paddy's with dad, I knew enough to showed mom how to play. She was a good cribbage and rummy player, and now she became addicted to poker. But poker isn't much fun with only two players, so mom got Clyde to play with us. Pretty soon the three of us were playing a lot of poker in the evenings. No money changed hands of course, we used match sticks instead of money. Sometimes dad joined in, which brought the average age of our gambling foursome to a legal eighteen (dad was thirty-two, mom was twenty-seven, I was seven and Clyde was six).

Paddy was a scary-looking character at the best of times, but in the dim light in the cluttered little shack, he was akin to the devil. The first couple of times I was there, I felt as if I had been 'pressed' aboard a pirate ship and was watching the crew plan a mutiny. Sitting in the dark with shadows from the flickering coal-oil lamps dancing across his craggy face and eye-patch, Paddy was the reincarnation of the villainous Long John Silver himself. All that was missing was a steel hook jutting from his shirt sleeve and a parrot on his shoulder.

In the light of day though, Paddy's appearance was any-thing but barbarous. Hopping across the sand with one leg and crutches he generated sympathy, not fear. The face that appeared so menacing in lantern light, was softened by a perpetual smile and cheery manner.

He was particularly nice to me and the other kids playing around the dock. And, he loved dogs. He had three of them including a mongrel female named Missy that he allowed inside even during the games. The other two stayed out and slept in a dog house at the side of his shack. I sat and played with Missy on the wooden floor whenever I got bored with the card game.

I don't know what the table stakes were but they couldn't have been very high. The antes (the initial bet before the deal) were made with pennies. Most of the coins in any pot were pennies and nickels. Paddy's poker games weren't for high rollers!

I imagine that the casinos in Reno, Carson City, and Las Vegas used poker chips in the 30s, but Paddy's game and others like it, were played with cash. poker chips didn't come into common use until plastics began to take over the world in the late forties. When a player ran out of coins Paddy made change out of a tobacco-can full of coins. It, and a couple more like it, sat on a wall shelf near the table. He kept one and two-dollar bills in a cigar box on the same shelf. Dad always worried that someone would break in and rob him. I didn't think so though. Paddy had a .38 revolver and let everybody know that he could, and would, use it.

He had also learned to use his right crutch as a weapon. He had drilled the bottom section our and filled it with lead and practiced swinging it around him like a martial artist's maru-bo staff.

"Nobody is ever going to hit me with pool cue or anything else again," he proclaimed. To make sure everybody knew it, he practiced daily; twirling his crutch on the sand where everyone could watch.

Empty tobacco cans played an important role, not only in

Paddy's casino, but in the whole of the Northern Ontario culture that we were a part of. We used them for everything from savings banks to spittoons and chamber pots.

Paddy always put one on the floor beside each player. They came in handy when the smoke from cigars, pipes, cigarettes, and coal oil lamps got so thick that nobody could read their cards. Although very few of the players chewed tobacco regularly, most of them switched to snuff or plug when the smoke got too bad. Then, of course, they had to spit somewhere.

'Tailor made' cigarettes were too expensive for the average person in the 1930s. Most men rolled their own. Large cans were the most economical packaging. My dad sometimes purchased 5-packs of "Turret" brand cigarettes for 5 cents, to treat himself at the end of a paperhanging job.

But, being only part-time chewers they didn't have much spitting practice. Most of them couldn't hit the insides of a washtub, let alone a four-inch tobacco can. By the time the games broke up, the floor would be a slimy, slippery, smelly mess of foul brown tobacco juice.

I don't know when or how Paddy cleaned it up, or even if he did, but it must have been some job with his one leg, crutches, and single eye. Maybe he paid one of the young wharf rats to do it for him.

Chewing tobacco is one of the most disgusting habits I can think of. Men – or women – who chew are easily distinguished by their dark brown slobber-stained chins, decayed and missing teeth, and putrid breath. It's hard to imagine intimacy between a woman and someone who chews. The mere thought of it is sickening.

I hated to be around anyone with that habit, but sometimes you just had to tighten up your stomach and put up with it. Dad didn't chew, but neither did he share my aversion to it. Sometimes he used a pinch of snuff when he was fishing, which In my book isn't an awful lot better. Anyway, the fact that his friend Mr. Trembley chewed Red Man Plug tobacco incessantly didn't bother him at all. He and the old man had been friends for years; ever since he went to school at Widdifield Station and he used to it.

Mr. Trembley (even my dad didn't know his first name) had often taken dad trout fishing in the creeks and streams that wound through Widdifield township, and had been very helpful and generous to dad's mother when she needed it. No amount of tobacco spit could stain my dad's high regard for him.

Chewing tobacco was the 'in' thing in the 1930s, and had side effects almost as devastating as those of crystal Meth, which has become so widely used by teenagers and young adults today. Both cause rotted-out teeth, disintegrated jaws, cancerous sores of the mouth and throat, and slow death. The big difference is that meth is addictive with the very first use, while chewing tobacco takes quite a bit of getting used to.

In the beginning, it is very difficult to recognize a recently addicted meth junky, while a chunk of tobacco being churned into a thick, slimy, expectorate by even a first-time user is apparent to everybody. First of all, the chew in his cheek bulges out the side of the his face, and, if that isn't evidence enough, he leaves behind him a trail of dirty brown sputum on roadways, sidewalks, and floors.

Mr. Trembley's teeth had rotted out long before I met him in 1937 and had been replaced by stainless steel dentures. Now he had developed cancer in his jaw and throat and didn't have long to live. Dad said he'd probably be dead in less than 6 months, and his prediction was right on. The old man died just before the daffodils bloomed in the spring of 1938.

A 'delicious' plug of Red Man Plug – one of the most popular brands in Northern Ontario in the 1930s

We saw him only one more time before he died. He showed up at our door on Timmins Street on a bitterly cold day just before Christmas 1937. His white hair was caked with ice and snow crystal, as were his bushy eyebrows, and the tip of his nose had a near-white pallor that spoke of frost-bite.

He had never been at our house before, or met my mother and siblings and his nervousness was apparent in his faltering words. "Hello Misses," he said through shivering lips. "I am Mr. Trembley from Widdifield. Is..does..Mister Herman Smith live here?"

"Yes. Please come in, Mr. Trembley," my mother said. "I am very happy to meet you. You are one of Herman's most treasured friends. You look half frozen."

She took his arm and led him into the house. Dad was already up from his chair, dragging it close to the wood stove in the center of the room, which was the only source of heat in our small four-room house. He rushed over to put his arm around his friend's shoulders and guide him to the chair.

"Hello, my old friend," he said. "I can't believe you came all this way in such bad weather. Please sit here while Ruth gets you a cup of hot tea. I'm sorry we have no whiskey. You look like you could use some."

"Cal, run out and get a handful of snow," dad told me. "Hurry! His nose is frost bitten. I think his ears are too." He rushed into the bedroom and got a quilt to put around the old man after he took the cold, wet coat off of him.

"I had to see you again Herman," the old man muttered and then grew quiet as dad bundled him up and began gently rubbing his nose and ears with the snow I'd brought in. It was a frost-bite treatment that I knew well, having had my own nose frozen a couple of time already. The snow prevents the tissues from thawing too quickly and resulting in permanent cell damage.

Mom came in with a bowl of home-made chicken soup. "Open wide, Mr. Trembley," she ordered. "This soup will fix what ails you."

He did as he was told, without reply and slurped down the broth she put into his mouth.

By the time she had fed him the bowl of soup and gave him a cup of sweetened tea, he had stopped shivering, but it was obvious that something was bothering him. We learned what it was a couple of minutes later after my mother left the room.

"Herman," he asked quietly; "would the misses mind if I chewed?"

"Of course not," dad replied. "You are our honored guest."

He told me to go and find an empty tobacco can that Mr. Trembley could use as a spittoon. We had a few of them under neath the kitchen sink. I got one and sat it beside the old man's chair. He spat into it a couple of times, then cut some chew from his plug and shoved it into his cheek with his tongue. Contented now, he settled back to enjoy the warmth of the fire and talk about the 'old days'.

As he chewed, he talked, and as he talked he spat. At first, he hit the can with unerring accuracy but as he grew warmer and the heat drove him back farther and farther from the stove, his under, and over, shoots began to outnumber the hits. But, neither he nor dad made any move to relocated the spittoon and a brown trail of spit soon extended halfway across the room.

If dad wasn't going to move the can, we kids certainly weren't going to touch it. Mom had excused herself earlier and was visiting Mrs. Doyle next door, so she couldn't do anything about it – at least, not right then.

What bothered me most was that dad usually got upset when any of us made the least bit of mess on the floor. Now, his disinterest in an even worse mess seemed a little bit unfair. Not because he didn't say anything to Mr. Trembley, but because he would leave it up to mom to clean the tobacco spit up later. "Isn't that what women are for?" he'd ask.

Mr. Trembley had come to tell dad that his doctor told him he had less than three months to live and that he would probably have to send him to the hospital soon to make sure he didn't suffer too much. He stayed with us for two days, and died in March, 1938.

Chapter Seventeen
THE DIONNE LEGACY

The Dionne Quintuplets, were born in the nearby village of Corbeil in 1934, becoming Ontario's greatest tourist attraction, drawing millions of visitors from around the world.

Because they were the only identical female quintuplets ever recorded, the provincial government had immediately recognized their commercial viability and acted quickly to make them "wards of the King", thus allowing them to take the children away from their parents and house them like animals in a zoo-like compound surrounded by a covered arcade. There, they were guarded night and day by three policemen, three nurses, two maids, a housekeeper, and four province-appointed guardians.

The Ontario tourism department promoted them heavily, building a very lucrative tourist industry around them. Over the next seven years the total revenue from them alone was more than $51 million – greater than the total farm income of any province in the country in that same time period.

The Quints were Ontario's number one attraction throughout their early childhood. More than three million people journeyed to North Bay between 1936 and 1943 to see the girls, more even, than visited the Canadian side of Niagara Falls.

The large influx of tourist to the region didn't stop when the show closed in 1943, because a large percentage of those who had come to see the little girls, had stayed to rent boats and fishing rods and thus discovered the magic of fishing in Lake

Nippissing.

They returned home with stories and pictures of huge fish that *"were so eager to be caught, they jumped into boat before you could get your hooks baited."* And the lake itself quickly became a tourist magnet. By 1938, North Bay was the most popular fishing destination in Eastern Canada.

Fishermen came in droves, bringing their friends and returning year-after-year to take home trophy-sized northern pike, bass, whitefish, muskies, sturgeon and perch. Mostly though, they came to fish for pickerel (walleye) which seemed to choke the lake with their large numbers. No fisherman ever got skunked.

Most of the visitors caught and kept a lot more fish than was legal – or reasonable. Many of them brought along portable canners and smokers to process their catch and thus get around possession limits. In spite of this massive over-fishing however, the lake proved so prolific that even the most outrageous activities have had little effect on the fish populations. Even today, fishermen take more than 200,000 walleyes from the 800 square miles of Lake Nippissing. The fishing just seems to get better and better.

Fishing from the North Bay dock never proved popular with visitors however. They preferred high speed boats, limber casting rods and Shakespeare's level-wind reels, to the boredom of still-fishing off a dock with bamboo poles and cotton line. But all the low-income residents who frequented the dock wanted, was easy access to the lake's almost limitless bounty. And here it was. Free to everyone!

The wharf was always crowded with men and boys fishing for perch, walleye pickerel, and northern pike. For the most part, their equipment consisted of 12-foot bamboo poles with heavy cotton fishing line tied around the narrow tip. Live minnows were impaled on J-shaped hooks and tossed twenty or thirty feet out into the water where a lead weight dragged them down to a depth of 15 to 20 feet, depending on where the carved wooden float had been tied to the line.

The Government dock in North Bay was built in the late 1800s to service the steamships that provided passenger service to Sturgeon Falls and the French River. It soon became a popular fishing spot for hundreds of local fishermen.

The methodology was primitive but effective. Very few fishermen ever went home without enough fish to feed his family a couple of hearty meals. Mostly, they caught four to six pound pickerel and that was just fine. Next to speckled trout, pickerel are by far Canada's most delicious fresh water fish. Pike were much bigger, but had too many small bones embedded in the flesh for comfortable eating. Perch were very tasty, but were seldom larger than a pound. There were plenty of bass in the lake, but not around the dock.

The wharf was big and jutted out well over 100 yards from shore. Still, in the 1930s, so many men had nothing more to do that fish, it was always crowded. If you wanted a prime spot on the dock where the largest schools hung out, you had to get there very early in the morning.

Chapter Eighteen
HONEY WAGON

I was only eight years old when my dad first took me fishing at the wharf. As we walked up the dock, he briefed me on what to expect.

"You're almost a man now, Cal," he had told me, "So don't go thinking I'm going to bait your hook, or take off the fish you catch. I'll show you how, but then you're on your own."

He didn't have to tell me that. In fact, I didn't want him to touch my fishing pole at all. I wanted to do it all myself. We had rigged up the poles the night before, and I'd laid awake for hours thinking about it.

"Ok dad," I said.

Even the mile walk to the dock along the lake from Timmins Street had been exciting. First of all, we had to pass by the hobo jungle and one of the men had spotted us before we got near. He cut us off before we got past.

"Hello mister," the hobo said. "Have you got a nickel for something to eat? I just got off a freight from Winnipeg and I haven't eaten for four days."

His story might have been true, but we didn't have enough for ourselves let alone for a panhandler, so dad made him an offer.

"I'd like to help you," he said, "but we don't have any

money either. Nor do we have any food, here or at home, and I have a wife a three kids to feed."

"But," he continued, "My son Cal here, and I, are on our way to go fishing at the city dock. If you'd like to come along, I think I can borrow a fishing pole for you, and maybe you can catch a couple of pickerel for your supper."

Dad said afterward that the response was always the same.

"I'd really like that," the man said. "But I've got to get to Ottawa and there's a freight coming through before noon that I might be able to hop. You wouldn't happen to have a fag (cigarette) on you, would you?"

Shortly after that encounter, we came to a big concrete block, maybe 20 feet across, built into the ground at the top of a sand cliff overlooking the lake. Its top poked about a foot out of the ground and there were four heavy round iron covers bolted onto it.

The whole place stunk like crazy and it sounded like a waterfall as we got near.

"What the heck is it?" I asked.

"It's where all the sewage from the west end of town comes together before it empties into the lake," he answered. "There are three of four others in town, but they aren't as big as this one. It's just like Chippewa Creek where it goes under that bridge at the beach near Ferris. We've passed by there many times."

I knew that place alright. We often crossed it on our way to visit Uncle Gordon and Aunt Jean. There was a story going around school about a little boy having drowned there some time earlier, but I didn't really believe it. The water stunk so bad that nobody would deliberately go anywhere near that creek. On the other hand, it emptied onto one edge of the beach where most of the people from the east end swam. So you never know.

In spite of the smell of the concrete sewer thing, I wanted to take a look and asked dad if I could.

"Well, if can stand the odor son, go right ahead, but I'll pass" he said. "Just hold your breath, and make it quick. Sewer gas is very dangerous."

He made me feel a lot better when he added, "There won't be any gas today with all that water rushing in, but get back here before you have to breathe anyway."

It was only 10 or fifteen feet to the closest cover so I took a deep breath and ran. looking down the the grating I saw a big concrete room half full of turbulent gray water, with three streams blasting more into it. I turned, ran back to dad, and let out my breath.

"Well, what did you see?" he asked.

"Nothing but stinky water," I replied. Then on second thought I asked, "Why do they have ladders going down there, dad?"

"Well," he answered, "some of the stuff in that water sinks down to the bottom of the tank. Eventually it gets too thick and has to cleaned out. That's when the sewer gas starts to build up and gets dangerous. One time, a couple of workers went down there and passed out. They would have died except they had safety ropes on and helpers up top pulled them out quickly and revived them. So whatever you do don't ever go near that place again, whether I'm with you or not."

He didn't have to tell me twice. I was already sick from the smell, but I had one more question: "Where does all that water go into the lake?"

He pointed down toward the dock. "There's a pipe under the water over there that takes it away out into the lake where it gets well-mixed with the water and doesn't bother anybody. There's a lot of sewer water going into the lake all the time. We've got 16,000 people in town and that's an awful of of crap!"

I didn't want to talk about it any more, but I wondered if the 'honey wagons' that hauled away the stuff away from our outdoor toilet dumped it somewhere out there too. I never did find out, even though I later got to know one of guys who did that for a living.

Stan McFarlane was a guitar player who performed occasionally in his brother Curly's country and western band. 'Curly McFarlane and his North Range Cowboys' was one the most famous dance bands in northern Ontario at the time and was featured on radio stations throughout the province. Stan is shown in the photo above as a boy, sitting in front of Curly in 1935, eight years before I got to know him.

Stan was married to Norma Jones, a sister of my best friend Ralph. They lived briefly with Norma's mother in a four room house on King Street north. Two other sisters Nina and Velma also lived there, as did their brothers George, Ralph, and Lloyd. A friend of Mrs. Jones and her 10-year old daughter shared a shed-like room attached to the kitchen. Stan and Norma slept with the rest of the family in any available space on the living room furniture or the floor.

What surprised me was how Stan always managed to stay so clean and odor-free in spite of his job emptying toilet cans into a horse-drawn wagon all day. But he did. And no one in the family seemed to think anything about it.

The cramped conditions of the Jones household were aggravated by the fact that Mrs. Jones occupied the only bedroom all by herself and remained there, locked in, day and night except when she had to empty her bed pot into the backyard outhouse, or make herself something to eat.

The place might have been disgusting, but it didn't bother me at all at the time. I was 13 then and had lived in slums and bush camps long enough to be oblivious to the cluttered mess and stayed there whenever I got the chance.

It's amazes me now how so many people could live reasonably normal lives like that. There were no family meals because there was no dining room, and the kitchen table was too small for more than two chairs. Consequently, everybody ate whatever they could find whenever they got hungry – although seldom anything other than toast and jam.

Bathing was done in a washtub in the kitchen, with blankets tacked over its two entrances and a shouted warning to "Keep out. I'm going to take a bath."

When one of the girls bathed, they had to post a guard to keep the boys from peeking. I had never seen a fully developed naked girl before and desperately wanted to see what they looked like. Particularly Nina, who was very buxom. She had laughed one time when she saw the naked girl I had drawn although she didn't tell me why. I never did get a glimpse of her without clothes, so I didn't know until much later that breasts had nipples.

Chapter Nineteen
THE PLAGUE

    Leaving the sewage aggregation site, we walked down the path onto the beach and arrived at the dock in time to get a spot that dad said was usually very productive. We set up our tin can place markers on the railing and unwound the line from the ends of our poles and prepared to bait the hooks. Dad took the perforated cover off the tin pail that we were using as a minnow bucket and took out a squirming, gasping little fish.

    "This is the dangerous part," he told me. "You have to hold the minnow very tightly so it can't wiggle while you put the hook through it's back. Otherwise you could hook your fingers instead."

    I looked with dismay at the little fish and gasped "No!" The fish wriggled in desperation. Dad saw the tears in my eyes and relented. He put the fish back in the can and without a word, stepped to the edge of the dock and poured all of the bait-fish back into the lake.

    "Maybe we can do just as well with worms," he suggested. "Shall we give it a try?" .

    "OK, dad," I agreed, pleased that we wouldn't have to use minnows today. "Worms don't have feeling, do they?"

    "Well not the same as animals and fish do anyway," he answered, and opened the worm can.

I didn't like hooking the dew worms much better. They had to be threaded onto the shaft of the hook and seemed even more frantic than the little minnow did. That's what attracts the fish, of course. "What cruel survival system this is," I thought. "We deliberately torture one poor creature, so we can kill and eat something else. What kind of a crazy thought up such a cruel system for animal survival?"

Anyway, I was part of it now and had no choice but to conform. Dad put the point of his hook through the worm and we were were ready to slaughter some fish.

I hadn't counted on spending a half hour getting the stupid hook into the water. It was a good thing we got there early and had plenty of room around us. I'm sure I would have caught me a fisherman by now.

"Hold it away back and toss it as hard as you can," dad instructed.

Well I already knew that, but knowing is different than doing. The hook dragged on the deck behind me on the first try and the worm got scraped off. Dad sacrificed another of the pathetically squirming creatures and shortened the line a bit. I tried again. This time I brought the rod tip over and down so far that the sinker and bait slapped the water together right below us. The worm came off again and a seagull ate it.

After a few more tries, I finally got the bait out far enough. The hook and sinker plummeted toward the bottom and would have gone all the way to the bottom if it hadn't been for the wooden 'bobber' tied fifteen feet up the line. In a few seconds the float sat floating quietly on the surface waiting for a fish to to take the bait.

"I knew you'd be a great fisherman, Cal," dad said. "Now just watch that float. When you see it dip underwater, grab the pole and jerk the tip up as high as you can."

I don't know how many times I saw the float dip underwater over the next half hour. Each time, I'd jerk the end of the pole up only to have dad tell me, "It must have got away, son. Or maybe one of those ripples pushed the float down. It's hard to tell the difference sometimes."

A little later, while he was busy getting us something to eat out of the lunch pail, I saw the float on his line suddenly disappear under the water. There was no mistaking it for a ripple this time. "Dad. You got a bite!" I screamed.

"Grab the pole for me Cal," he said, "Just jerk the tip up. I'll take over when I can."

Excitedly, I lifted his fishing pole and flipped the tip up as hard as I could. The rod bent and I felt something struggling on the other end of the line. I had never experienced anything like it in my life before. I couldn't see what it was, but it was jerking on my arms like an angry shark. Not that I knew what a shark felt like.

"It's really big, Dad," I yelled. "What should I do?"

"Just keep the line tight, son," he replied calmly. "I'll be there in a minute."

The fish was moving back and forth and I could see the line cutting through the water. "He's getting away," I screamed. What should I do?"

A few fishermen had gathered around, attracted by my excited shouts. One said, "you're doing fine lad. Just keep the line tight and stay calm. You've got him."

I pulled harder and then Dad was at my elbow. "OK, son," he told me. "You caught him, so you have to get him in. Just start pulling the pole backwards, hand-over-hand, until you can catch hold of the line. Then you can lift him onto the dock."

The rest was easy. I got the line in one hand and started pulling it up. The fish came struggling out of the water. A few seconds later it was flapping on the dock – a great big six pound pickerel. I felt hands clapping me on the back and looked around proudly at the men who had gathered around to watch.

My Dad grinned. "That's my son," he announced, as he removed the fish from the hook and clubbed it on the head.

"We have to do that to kill it quickly," he explained when he say my pained expression. "Otherwise it would suffer a long time for nothing."

"Oh!" I said. "But I don't want to kill any more fish Dad."

"Well go and ask Paddy if he has something you can put enough water in to keep the next ones alive in," he suggested. "It has to have two handles so we can carry it home."

Paddy gave me an old galvanized wash tub, into which I later put a small grass pike and a pickerel. But they both died before we left the wharf. Probably from the soap residue in the tub, dad explained. He put them on the stringer with his fish to eat for supper.

I took the tub back to Paddy while dad was getting ready to go, and told him about the other two fish I had caught.

"You're gonna be a world champion fisherman one of these days," he told me. "Ain't no doubt about it. You go over to the cooler there and grab yourself a pop. You earned it! And bring one for me too."

When I returned with the pop, we sat down on his 'thinking log'.

"How many fish are in the lake anyway, Paddy?" I asked as I handed him a bottle. "There must be an awful lot."

"Well boy, there ain't no way of telling exactly, but this

lake ain't ever liable to run out of fish in spite of all the Yankees. There are very few lakes like this anywhere in the world. Most would have been fished out years ago with the number of greedy tourists that we get coming up here every year; trolling and netting, and canning and smoking everything they get, so's to get around our maximum possession limits."

"How come there's still so many fish then?" I wondered.

"Well it's just like them shadflies everybody gets so excited about," he answered. "There are just too darn many of them. No matter how many you catch, there's another crop just waiting to be hatched."

I didn't know if 'too darn many of them' referred to fish or the large but harmless mayflies that plague the city for three weeks between late June and mid-July every year. They arrive by the billions covering everything in smothering blankets of their gray, semi-transparent bodies. Clouds of them dance around street lights and neon signs, accumulating like snow drifts in front of stores, while their owners try unsuccessfully to maintain shad-free paths for their customers.

The insects would be quite welcome if it wasn't for their large size and overwhelming numbers. They have no mouths or stingers, and are quite harmless. Nor do they come into town deliberately. A small percentage of the countless numbers that come to surface of the lake to mate become confused by the city lights and head for town where they quickly and thickly carpet roadways, sidewalks, buildings, walls, windows, and pedestrians. Even a tiny percentage of trillions is an awful lot of shadflies. .

One year, they were so thick that the head of the Downtown Improvement association even considered conscripting residents to stand on Main street with feather dusters to brush them off shoppers. It would have been a better idea to declare a dusk to dawn blackout instead, because of the flies' suicidal attraction to light. If it wasn't for city lights shadflies would be more than content to stay on the lake doing nothing but mating for their last three days and nights on earth.

Although the billions of shadflies that die in the city never reproduce, countless other billions remain over the water, and for three weeks the surface of the lake becomes a veritable soup of shadfly bodies and eggs. The main expanse of the beaches remain relatively free of them, but the waterline is fouled with a long, thick line of their rotting carcasses. The stench keeps would-be bathers away until August, when mother nature has had time to clean up the mess

Paddy said that shadflies are the most important creatures in the lake – at least as far as fish are concerned. Their nymphs live on the bottom for three years before they reach maturity. Then, when they swim to the surface, they unfold their wings and spend three days mating and molting, after which every single one of them dies. However, by the time the mating season is over, most of females will have laid up to 8,000 eggs each on the surface of the lake. Shortly afterward trillions more shadfly larvae sink to the bottom to become predatory nymphs, constantly feeding and being fed upon.

He also told me that the reason other lakes don't have nearly as many shadflies as Nippissing does, is the lake's great size – it's the fifth lake in the province – not counting the five Great Lakes – and has an unusually shallow bottom. Very few parts of the lake are deeper than thirty feet. Consequently, the water is very warm in summer and cold in winter, creating convection currents that keep the water exceptionally well aerated, so creating an abnormally healthy habitat for a rich variety of animal and plant life. More than 30 species of fish, and numerous crustaceans, abound in its waters.

According to the July 2002, edition of the North Bay Nugget, Dr. Reid Taylor of Manitoba, has been dining on shadflies for years.

"The insects taste like fish," Dr. Tayor told the Nugget. "If you munch a handful, they have the texture of breakfast food."

I wonder if Doctor Taylor likes earthworms too?

It seemed as if the breezes brought them,
It seemed as if the seagulls taught them.
As if the lights were mates they knew
Quickly into town they flew.

Chapter Twenty

QUICKSAND

Automobiles came into the Smith family's lives for the first time, on Timmins Street in 1937, in the form of an old 1918 Ford 'Tin Lizzie'. The 'T' may have been America's first affordable automobile, but that tribute was for Fords in general, not the junker that dad brought home. This one was 19 years old and ready for the scrap heap.

It made the poem about Henry Ford seem almost understated:

> "There was a little man,
> His name was Henry Ford.
> He took a piece of tin
> And a little bit of board.
> He had a drop of gas
> In an old tin can,
> When he put it all together,
> The damn thing ran."

Dad bought the car mostly for picking blueberries. He was tired of hitch-hiking 15 or 20 miles to and from the berry patch. But this thing was a pure waste of money. It never did get us to a berry patch, and rarely made it more than a few blocks from home. Its natural rubber tubes and tires were so old and rotten that they seldom lasted more than a mile or two before dad had to pull them off the rims and patch them again. Worse than that, the engine wouldn't start with making a serious attempt to break his arm with the crank handle.

Just try to imagine driving something with tires that blow out every hundred yards, and an engine that has to be cranked by hand and tries to break your arm all the time.

The luxurious cab of our 1918 Model T.

Dad seemed happy with it though, at least for the first couple of days. After a few painful bruises, he had learned to retard the spark (whatever that means) before touching the crank. I guess it meant setting the spark weak enough to match the mentality of the the person who was retarded enough to buy such a machine in the first place.

It was also important for the operator to understand that the handbrake was used to put the car in reverse, and that the foot brake shouldn't be used in slick conditions because it operates a band around the transmission, not the drum brakes, which can put the car into a dangerous skid.

Whew! Are you still with me?

All that gobledegook might not make sense to you, but it

did to dad, so one sunny day we loaded the back seat with Clyde, Jeri, me, and a dozen big berry baskets. Charlotte was too young for such a long journey in a car like this, and was staying with Irene Filiatreau. Mom got in the front seat with dad.

We got to the north edge of town and began the mile long drive up Thibeault Hill. The car tackled the hill as if it really intended to go to the top. But by the time we were half way up, it had clearly lost its resolve and was moving like a teenager who had been asked to take the garbage out. By the time we got within 50 yards of the summit, a scant few feet lower than the peak of Mount Everest you understand, you'd swear it had a pain in its air filter.

Two hitchhikers at the top of the hill had been watching our ascent. At first with hands raised high, thumbs up, eagerly hoping we'd see them and offer a ride. Now, they were sitting on their back packs hoping we wouldn't see them and ask them to push.

Then, just when the car seemed to be gasping its last breath, the slope began to flatten and the wheels started turning a little faster. By the time we reached the hitch-hikers our speed had increased to five miles per hour. We had made it. The two men stood up and began to clap and cheer for our marvelous victory over this seemingly insurmountable hill. Or were they cheering because they saw that we didn't have room to give them a ride?

Dad waved at them and took a bow, then made a sharp U-turn, shut off the engine, and coasted back down to town.

For a while after he got rid of the Model T, dad rode a bicycle. He had started working with mom's brother Clifford, hanging paper soon after his back wound healed. But the job ended just before Christmas when Cliff went to Buffalo to work with his brother Earl, who had won a big painting contract in a new low-income housing project there.

Before he left, Clifford gave dad a couple of papering contracts that he had negotiated, but no tools to work with. Fortunately, the local paint and wallpaper dealer agreed to give him the basic tools and supplies he needed. The more expensive items – pasting table, ladders, and extension planks – dad could make by hand. The pasting table that he built was fabulous. It was seven feet long and three feet wide, but folded into a long thin box, in which he could carry his brushes, trimmers, yardsticks and other small implements. The ladders and extension planks were sturdy, but light enough to make transport easy. He was still using them when I joined the Canadian air force in August, 1950.

Having no means of moving his equipment from job to job, he arranged to have Deluxe Taxi to it for him. Payment was to be made on move-out, when the jobs were finished and he had settled up with his customers. He himself rode back and forth to work on a bicycle to save extra taxi costs.

Everything must have worked out OK, because he bought a 1928 Plymouth sedan the following summer, primarily so we could go picking blueberries between paperhanging jobs and make some extra money. So, when he announced one evening that the berries were ripe and we'd be going to Sand Dam first thing next morning, everybody was excited. We were going on our first trip in our new car. First in any car if you don't include the Thibeault Hill fiasco.

I don't know why we called the place Sand Dam, there was no dam there. In fact, there was nothing except a tunnel under the highway through which Duchesnay Creek drained a nearby string of small lakes and thousands of acres of wet land into Lake Nippissing, twenty miles away.

A fire had swept the area on the downstream side of the highway two years earlier, and now the area was thick with low-bush blueberries. They are one of the few plants that can withstand the high temperatures of a forest fire.

Then in the fire's aftermath, when the ground is rich with charcoal and ash, the seeds split open and a new crop of blueberry bushes turns the hillsides green. Pine, spruce, and birch tree cones are also split by the heat, and spring to life to compete with the berry bushes for footing in the burned out terrain. At first, the blueberry bushes dominate, but within a few years, the trees grow tall and rob the bushes of the intense sunlight they need for survival. The plants gradually die out, but their seeds live on, remaining dormant until they are exposed to the heat of another fire.

We drove up a disused logging road through the treeless landscape until we were stopped by a large log across the road, a few feet away from a small shallow stream. Alder bushes had already grown tall along the stream, shading the area and making it a perfect place for our parents to leave us while they picked berries on the nearby slopes.

Clyde and I had stacks of comic books to read, and slingshots to practice with when we got bored with Captain Marvel, Plastic Man, and the other super heroes. We had built a good collection of comics by trading the protective ends that dad knocked off of wallpaper rolls for them. The discs of rolled paper made great throwing missiles; unrolling and dragging long paper streamers behind them.

Pretty soon though, every clothesline, telephone wire, power line, and tree in the entire neighborhood was aflutter with paper streamers, and our comic trading enterprise was brought to a halt by a visit from Constable Green who asked my dad if he would mind giving the kids something else to play with – which was OK by me. By then we had a large enough inventory of comic book 'traders' to give us a never-ending supply of fresh reading material.

Jeri and Tweet (Charlotte) were fully occupied with dolls,

board games, and the knitting spools dad had made for them. In the past month Jeri had produced two hot-pot pads from yarn that she'd unraveled from worn-out sweaters. Charlotte had a yard or so of knitted tubing that she insisted was going to be a rug for the side of the bed she and Jeri shared at home.

Clyde had proudly brought along the camera he'd earned selling subscriptions to 'The Saturday Evening Post'. The only problem was he didn't have any film. Dad couldn't afford it. But he liked clicking the shutter anyway.

We were in an area of low, apparently logged-off hills filled with blackened stumps and small fallen logs, but no trees – burned or otherwise. Dad said it probably meant the fire had been a slash fire, deliberately set by the company that logged off the trees. It certainly looked that way.

Knitting spools produce long tubes of yarn that can be coiled to produce doilies, place mats, and rugs.

They left us at the car, crossed the tiny stream, and followed the old logging road up and around the edge of the hill and disappeared with their empty berry baskets. When they returned sometime around ten o'clock, all of the 11-quart baskets filled to heaping with big, delicious-looking berries.

We all gathered around them excitedly, eyeing the berries. "Can we have some," we begged.

"No berries for kids," Mom said. "There are tons of them right around here that you kids can pick. These are for sale so we can buy some real food at home."

"Let's have some sandwiches," dad interjected, "then

you can all go and eat some right off the bushes. There are lots right here near the car. Maybe you can fill a couple of small baskets to take home so mom can make us a couple of blueberry pies tomorrow. How does that sound?"

It sounded good to me.

"How about it, Clyde?" I asked. "There are some one-quart boxes in the car. Maybe we ca fill a couple of them."

Clyde didn't answer, but Jeri was excited about the idea.

"I'll go with you, Cal. I love picking berries." she said.

Mom had already got the lunch basket that dad had tied to an alder limb to keep it cool and out of reach of ants and bugs. we spread an old cloth on the hood of the car and stood around eating scrambled egg and bologna sandwiches. I went to the little stream on the other side of the log and brought back a can of cool, clear water which we all drank from. Dad said the stream was one of many small tributaries of the same Duchesnay Creek that flowed into Lake Nippissing, a mile or so west of our house on Timmins Street.

After lunch mom and dad left with more empty baskets. When they were out of sight, I asked, "Who wants to go and pick some berries now?"

"Not me," said Charlotte, "I'm too small."

"Not me either," Clyde grumbled. "I'm staying here to look after Charlotte."

"OK," I said to Jeri, "I'll get a couple of baskets and we'll go by ourselves."

She nodded and told Charlotte she wouldn't be far away and would be back soon.

In fact, we weren't more than fifty feet away before we

found a large patch of berries and began to pick. As soon as we cleaned that one out, we got into another, then another, and another. I began to wonder why mom and dad went over the hill when they could have picked right here.

The more I thought about it, the more suspicious I got. I remembered the story about Hansel and Gretel and how their parents took them into the woods, then left them and went home without them. Maybe mom and dad were trying to do the same with us kids. Maybe they were in the hills watching and waiting for us to get far enough away from the car so they could sneak down and drive off.

When I couldn't stand it any longer, I asked Jeri what she thought about it. She said I was being silly.

"Mom would never leave Clyde," she said. "She likes him too much. And Charlotte's her little baby."

"But what about you and I?" I asked. "We're nobody's favorites. Maybe we shouldn't get too far away from the car."

She hesitated now. She hadn't thought about that. So now both us were worried. A few minutes later, she showed me her berry basket.

"I think I have enough now Cal," she said anxiously. "How about you?"

"Yes," I answered, and we headed for the car.

Mom and dad came back, of course, and told us to get all of our stuff into the car. We were going to the pool to eat lunch. They were referring to the small widening in Duchesnay Creek near the tunnel under the Trans Canada highway.

The first time we came up here to pick blueberries, we'd looked for a swimming hole, but the biggest pool we could find that was convenient to the highway was only about three feet deep and eight feet across. Rivers and Creeks are usually much smaller at their sources, so it wasn't surprising to find no pools up here you could rightly call 'swimming holes' like the one under the railway bridge near town.

It was a great spot for a picnic though, so mom and dad had decided to stop there today and eat what was left of our lunch before driving back to town. They said they needed to relax and rest their backs after spending all day bent over like a couple of coolies in a rice paddy.

The water in the pool was just like spring water – clear enough to see little fish swimming over the white-sand bottom.

"It's a nice place for little fish," dad observed, "but it's not nearly deep enough for us to swim in – although if we had our bathing suits, it'd be a good place to cool off before heading back to town."

"I'll bring them next time," mom said, unaware that the fine white sand that looked so inviting was one of Mother Nature's most terrifying man traps – quicksand!

We went back to Sand Dam a couple of days later and returned to the pool again to have lunch after mom and dad finished picking berries. We kids ate hurriedly and changed into our bathing suits, one at a time, in the shelter of the car doors. Being the fastest eater in the family, I was the first one ready to test the water, but dad stopped me from going in.

"Stay right here until everybody's ready." he ordered. "You never know. The pool could be full of leaches, or water snakes, or who knows what else. Never go into strange water alone."

Finally, with everyone ready to go, I appointed myself official pool-tester and dove into the shallow water head first while everyone watched. The momentum carried me easily, just under the surface, to the other side of the small pool, where I turned, still underwater, and swam back to where I started. The water was great. But where I raised my head for air and tried to stand up, my feet sank into the sandy bottom. It was like being stuck in a bowl of thick jelly. With no support for my feet I couldn't straighten up. I was trapped face down in the water struggling frantically to keep my head above the surface. Thank God, dad had stopped me from going into the pool alone. If he hadn't been right there to grab my arms and drag me ashore I would have drowned for sure.

Clyde, Jeri, me, and Dad on the bank of Dushesnay Creek at Sand Dam. The dusty two-lane gravel Trans Canada Highway can be seen in the background.

As we learned that day, part of quicksand's menace is its deceptive appearance. It looks like firm, solid ground – whether it's sand, silt, clay, or any other grainy soil – but it isn't. Under certain conditions the individual grains of sand are held suspended in a pocket of water and develops the consistency of wet concrete. It seldom happens in lakes, rivers or creeks, but when it does, it usually forms along the inside bend, near shore, as was the case at Sand Dam. It can also happen in shallow pools, sand washes, swamps, and canyons fed by spring water.

The common misconception is that quicksand drags you down until your head goes under and you drown. Such is not the case. Flesh and blood is only half as dense as quicksand and you won't sink much below your knees. Entrapment usually occurs on 'dry' land where you can just lay back, spread your weight out and slowly back stroke to firmer ground. If you happen to fall forward however, it takes a lot of effort to keep your head 'above water' and suffocating becomes a real possibility. The key to survival, as in any dangerous situation, is in staying calm.

Somehow, the quicksand trap at Sand Dam made our subsequent picnics there even more fascinating. Now the pool took on the same evil, fascination that the sirens of Greek mythology had for the sailors they lured to their doom on the rocky shores of their island of Anthemoessa. But we, like the Argonauts who sailed by the island unharmed, could enjoy the music and leave anytime we wanted to.

Jeri was only six years old at that time, but she was more responsible than most adults and I liked picking berries with her. We didn't talk much. It was just nice being together. She was a very pretty little girl, with a quiet, pleasant disposition and was quick to offer help with any chore our parents gave me. I was usually good to her as well, although sometimes I teased a little too much - especially about her lips which she believed were too big.

Actually, they weren't big, just full. They made her look a lot like Gina Lollobrigida when she got older. Still, Clyde and I teased her unmercifully, saying she looked like one of those African women with the plates in their lips that we saw once in a

National Geographic Magazine.

To this day Jeri is very beautiful. But her ego took a hit a few years ago while she was visiting her son Jamie and his family in the Yukon.

She was entertaining her five-year-old grandson Mathew in the guest room just before dinner and decided she should change her clothes.

"I'm sorry, Mathew," she told him. "You'll have to go out for a couple of minutes. Granny needs to change her clothes."

Mathew didn't want to go. "Please let me stay, Granny," he pleaded.

"No sweetheart," she said. "I have to undress and little boys need to leave."

"But Granny," he begged. "Please don't make me go. I promise I won't laugh."

Charlotte and Jeri both worked as Bell Telephone Operators in North Bay during their teen-age years. Jeri became a supervisor and retired in 2000 after 40 years with the company.

Cal and Jeri – December 2009 Ages 80 and 78

My mother beside our house on Harriet Street

Jeri and dad, hamming it up at our farm in 1946.

Our home in the bush behind the North Bay airport on Smith Road. So named because we were the only family on that road in the 1940s.

My Mother shot a weasel in one of the trees in the background. We skinned it and sold the fur to the Nippissing Raw Fur company for 50 cents.

Keeping clean in the poor neighborhoods of North Bay and its surrounds was difficult. Some of the houses we lived in during the 'Dirty 30s' had no running water. It had to be dipped out wells or spring fed streams. There were no indoor toilets, and the outhouses were not heated – even in minus 20F temperatures. Those houses that did have running water, had no way to heat it, other than on top of a wood stove like the one above.

Manufactured by Amazon.ca
Bolton, ON

39305720R00095